The Complete

CAT

OWNER'S MANUAL

The Complete
CAT
OWNER'S MANUAL

SUSIE PAGE

FOG CITY PRESS

Published by Fog City Press
814 Montgomery Street
San Francisco, CA 94133 USA

Conceived and produced by Weldon Owen Pty Limited
59 Victoria Street, McMahons Point, NSW, 2060, Australia
A member of the Weldon Owen Group of Companies
Sydney • San Francisco

Reprinted 2003

FOG CITY PRESS
Chief Executive Officer: John Owen
President: Terry Newell
Publisher: Lynn Humphries
Managing Editor: Janine Flew
Design Manager: Helen Perks
Editorial Coordinator: Kiren Thandi
Production Manager: Caroline Webber
Production Coordinator: James Blackman
Salaes Manager: Emily Jahn
Vice President International Sales: Stuart Laurence

Project Editor: Libby Frederico
Designer: Kylie Mulquin
Picture Researcher: Karen Burgess

A Guide to Breeds by Lynn Cole and Susie Page
The Cat and its Relatives by Susan Lumpkin and John Seidensticker

THE IAMS COMPANY
The Iams Company, makers of Eukanuba® and Iams® Cat
and Dog Foods, has a vision to be recognized as the world leader
in cat and dog nutrition. With a strong foundation of core beliefs
about culture, customers, products and people, The Iams Company
is committed to enhancing the well-being of cats and dogs by
providing world-class quality foods.

Iams, Eukanuba, the paw print design, and the composite Iams Company
and paw print design are trademarks of The Iams Company registered
in the U.S. Patent and Trademark Office. The color rhodamine red
is a trademark of The Iams Company.

For more information about the care and feeding of your pets, contact
The Iams Company at 1-800-525-4267 or www.iams.com.

A catalog record for this book is available from the
Library of Congress, Washington, DC.

ISBN 1 875137 84 X

Color reproduction by Colourscan Co Pte Ltd.
Printed by Leefung-Asco Printers
Printed in China

A Weldon Owen Production

CONTENTS

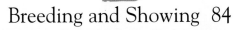

INTRODUCTION

Having a cat can do wonders for a person's health and happiness. It can reduce stress and help us lead longer, fuller lives. The unconditional love and companionship from your cat create a true friend for life. Today millions of proud cat owners around the world are testimony to this unique relationship.

The Complete Cat Owner's Manual provides present and prospective cat owners with the information they need to care for their pet. From choosing the right cat, to feeding tips, to health care essentials, this book is filled with sound, practical advice. Also included is a detailed guide to more than 35 of the world's most popular cat breeds, providing helpful information about the lifestyles and lifestages of those breeds.

For those people who already own a cat, this book will be an invaluable reference for the whole family. For those who are deciding what kind of cat would best suit their lives, it will be an inspiration. Remember, owning a cat is a genuine responsibility, and we must ensure that every care is taken to make our cats' lives as happy as possible. Your efforts will be rewarded with years of friendship and love.

From the cat lovers at The Iams Company

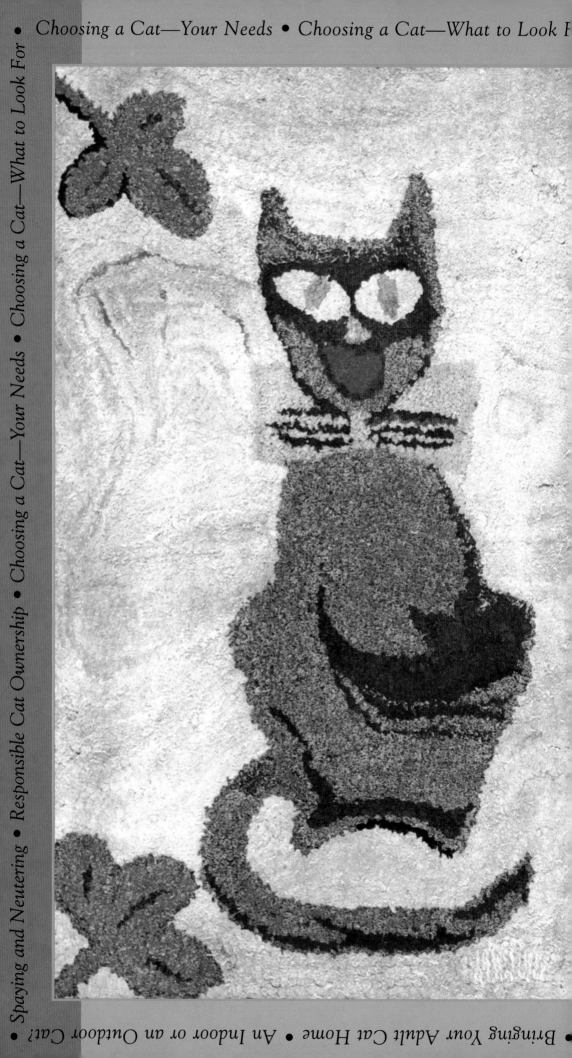

YOU AND YOUR CAT

To gain the friendship of a cat is a difficult thing. The cat is a philosophical, methodical, quiet animal, tenacious of its own habits, fond of order and cleanliness, and it does not lightly confer its friendship. If you are worthy of its affection, a cat will be your friend, but never your slave. He keeps his free will, though he loves, and he will not do for you what he thinks is unreasonable. But if he once gives himself to you it is with absolute confidence and affection.

THÉOPHILE GAUTIER (1811-1872),
French poet and novelist

CHOOSING A CAT— YOUR NEEDS

Are you looking for a buddy or a companion cat? Or are you interested in breeding and showing cats? Only a very small percentage of cat owners want to breed and exhibit their cats. Most are looking for that special cat to share their heart and home.

STARTING OUT

A new kitten is the beginning of a wonderful friendship. Just be certain that you and your family can afford the time and money needed to care for him properly.

Before you acquire a cat, ask yourself if you are willing and able to provide for him for some 18 years or more. Do you have a safe environment in which he can live? Do you have the time to groom and care for him? Are your children trained in the responsibilities of pet ownership? Are your other pets willing to accept a newcomer?

If you answer yes to these questions, then ask yourself if you can afford a cat. The initial cost of a kitten or cat is nothing compared with the ongoing costs of keeping him safe and healthy. You must be sure you can afford to feed him, as well as keep him current on his vaccinations, yearly physicals and any other veterinary care he may need. If you are still answering yes, rest assured that the time and money you spend will be repaid a hundred times by the companionship and love he will give you.

It doesn't matter how large or small your house is—cats fit anywhere and so any type of home will do. Most pet owners live in cities and are apartment dwellers, and the absence of a yard is not a problem. All cats can adapt to life indoors. Even if they object at first, simply ignore their pleas to go outside and they will eventually quiet down. If you live in an area where your cat is safe outdoors, then any yard is big enough for his needs.

KITTEN OR ADULT

There are many adult cats that, for various reasons, need to find loving homes. It's not always easy adopting an adult, but the affection you reap will be well worth your patience. Kittens, on the other hand, are easier to adopt as they adapt more readily. If you have other cats in your home, they may adjust more

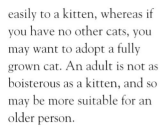

easily to a kitten, whereas if you have no other cats, you may want to adopt a fully grown cat. An adult is not as boisterous as a kitten, and so may be more suitable for an older person.

PUREBRED OR NOT?
There are more mixed-breed cats in the world than purebreds. And Mother Nature often does a better job of painting them more beautifully than many of the pedigreed cats.

The main advantage of acquiring a pedigreed cat is that he will be more likely to live up to the breed characteristics and quirks that you may desire. Certain purebreds may appeal to you because of their color, coat or composition and, if this is important to you, then a pedigreed cat is for you.

If you just want a cat to be your friend and playmate, then any cat, pedigreed or mixed-breed, will fit the bill. A cat doesn't know or care if he has a pedigree. Cats eat

like cats, play like cats and love us like cats, no matter where they come from. You can't go wrong bringing any kind of cat into your life.

CHOOSING
A BREED
There are many considerations to take into account when choosing a breed. Those Persian cats with baby-doll faces and long, flowing coats may appeal to you, but do you have the time and the inclination to groom them each and every day? A day without combing this kind of coat is an invitation to tangles and matting. A happy compromise enabling you to have that doll-like Persian face coupled with a short coat that requires less grooming is the Exotic Shorthair. In the United Kingdom, a similar type of cat is called the British Shorthair, and in mainland Europe it is called the European Shorthair.

DAILY CARE
If you're buying a longhaired cat, such as this Persian, be prepared to put aside time every day to groom him.

LIFE AT THE TOP
Don't worry about how little room you have, or whether you live in a house or a high-rise apartment; a cat will quickly adapt to his new environment. All you need to do is ensure it is safe.

MIXED-BREED OR PEDIGREED
Unless you are wanting specific characteristics in your cat, or are planning to breed, you should consider acquiring a mixed-breed.

CLIMATE CONTROL

When choosing a cat, give careful consideration to which breeds are suited to your climate. Those with little hair, such as this Cornish Rex, will need special care in keeping them warm and free from drafts.

Are you a person who likes peace and quiet? Then perhaps neither the Siamese nor the Oriental Shorthair is for you because their voices can be very loud. And if you want your curios to remain on their shelves or the coffee table, then most of the shorthaired breeds are taboo. They just love to rearrange anything movable.

A Guide to Breeds (starting on p. 116) will help you decide which cat best suits you, your lifestyle and your family needs.

MEETING THE FAMILY

When you bring your new cat home, make sure he is given plenty of time to adjust to his new surroundings before he meets his new playmates.

CLIMATE

Do you live in a place that's hot and humid? If so, a longhaired breed may not be comfortable unless you have air-conditioning. And a shorthaired cat could shiver his days away in a cold and windy climate, unless kept strictly indoors. Even then, he will want the furnace going because he doesn't have a thick coat to keep him warm.

Certain breeds, such as the Sphynx (see p. 204) and Rexes (see pp. 148–151), have little or no hair and need special handling. The Sphynx can be easily sunburned too, so must be sheltered from sunlight.

A LAP-CAT

Not every cat will sit on your lap. Some are too busy or too highly strung to settle down for long. Others, that have thick or long coats, may not like the added warmth of our laps. It makes them feel uncomfortable and they move away. Since all cats are lap-size, if you really want to increase your chances of him being a lap-cat, a shorthaired cat is for you, but there are no guarantees.

CATS FOR CHILDREN

Cats and children mix very well with a little help from you. It is important that children be taught the proper way to interact with cats. Although a kitten may have a hard time escaping the tail-pulling and hair-yanking inflicted by a toddler, an older cat will simply move away if playtime turns into wartime. And most cats are quite forgiving of children and will tolerate being held in all sorts

SURVIVAL SKILLS
If you want your cat to be an indoor/outdoor cat, you should be aware that he may remain very independent and not become the doting companion you expected.

CHOOSING A
VETERINARIAN

of undignified positions. Let an adult try to hold him with his head dangling down and he will react with outrage, but a child can carry him any which way and he loves it.

If you are bringing a kitten into a house with children, encourage the children to stay away from the kitten until he approaches them. And make sure there is proper supervision until you are confident they are mixing together safely.

Indoor or Outdoor
An indoor/outdoor cat may be more independent because he will use his wild instincts for survival. A completely indoor cat may surprise you by shedding his independent nature and becoming almost dog-like in his responses to you. Your best bet in selecting your ideal cat is simply to pick one that you like the

look of, keeping in mind any special grooming he may require, and trust the way you respond to his "personality." You can then gradually integrate him into your household routine.

One Too Many
Don't make the mistake of adding one too many cats to your household. Whether two is company and three is a crowd, or whether your cat household will tolerate more cats is up to your cats. They have a silent agreement as to the number of cats they feel can coexist in any one household and they will let you know as soon as you have exceeded that limit in any number of ways—from simple acts such as wetting your bedspread, all the way to physically attacking the unwanted newcomer.

When choosing a veterinarian, it is not only important to find one who likes cats but also to find one who will work with you in keeping your pet healthy. It is important to locate a veterinarian who is technically competent and with whom you feel comfortable. After all, it is you who lives with your cat and knows his normal behavior. Unless your cat is sick, you will probably need to take him to the veterinarian only once each year for his checkup and annual booster vaccinations.

MAKING FRIENDS
Although they may not warm to each other immediately, give your pets time to get to know each other, and after a little while they should be the best of friends.

CHOOSING A CAT — WHAT TO LOOK FOR

Now that you have decided you want a cat as a pet and have chosen the type of cat you'd love to have, you need to make sure you find the right cat from the right place.

THE ONCE OVER

Before purchasing a kitten or cat, be sure to check that he is fit and healthy. Don't forget to take a peek inside his ears to make sure he doesn't have ear mites.

When you choose that special kitten or cat, you want him to be as fit as possible. His eyes should be clear. His nose should not be runny. Run your hands gently down his back and across his hips. He should have enough flesh covering him that you don't feel his backbone and hip bones. His coat should feel clean. If your cat is a shorthair, his coat should lie flat and not be dull and open, and if he is a longhaired cat, it should be full-bodied and not dry. He should not have bad breath and ideally should have no odor. In a kitten, especially, lightly finger his stomach to make sure it is not distended or out of proportion to the rest of his body.

When handling a strange kitten or cat, do not pick him up and hold him up in the air. This often frightens him and he will react by crying and trying to escape. Stoop down to his level and place him on your lap to examine him.

WHERE TO FIND
Kittens and cats can be found abandoned and hiding under cars or bushes. They can be acquired from local animal shelters or by contacting cat rescue groups. These sources, however, will not be able to provide you with details of the cat's parents, ancestors, or any possible hereditary defects.

Local newspapers and notices on veterinarians' bulletin boards may also list available kittens and cats. Pet stores are another source.

THE CORRECT WAY TO HOLD A CAT

You can safely pick up a kitten by the scruff of the neck, while at the same time supporting him by placing your hand underneath his body. However, never pick up an adult cat this way.

To pick up an older kitten or a small cat, support his weight from underneath with one hand and hold him securely to your chest with the other hand. If he is a larger cat, pick him up by placing one arm under his body from the rear, with your hand coming up between his front legs. Support his weight with the other hand and hold him firmly to prevent him from freeing himself.

Never pick a cat up by his leg or his tail, and don't let children pick him up this way either. A child and a cat will usually work out an equitable solution. The cat may simply let himself go limp and allow the child to carry him around plopped over the child's arms with the rest of him dangling.

Check to ensure that the animals are kept in sanitary conditions, are in good health, and that the pet store guarantees the health of animals it sells.

Purebred cats are also available through private breeders and catteries. They are also offered for sale—or adoption in the case of older, retired breeding cats—at cat shows. Cat magazines carry listings of breeders and venues of cat shows and are a good source for locating cats.

When buying a cat from a breeder, let your first impression be your guide. If there is a strong odor in the house, or if the cats flee in fright, then you should not purchase a kitten or cat there. Although most cats will hide temporarily when strangers invade their homes, the well-adjusted cat will soon emerge from hiding to explore the new person. Nothing is more curious than a cat. It's also a good idea to see the parents of the kitten as this will give you some idea of his size and appearance when fully grown.

If the house or the litter pans are not clean, then the chances are high the kitten will not be clean either.

PAPERWORK

Be sure to receive a record of your kitten's vaccinations. If you are acquiring a pedigreed cat for breeding, you will need his pedigree and registration certificates as well.

BRINGING YOUR NEW KITTEN HOME

*Now the exciting moment has arrived for both you and your kitten.
Be aware, though, that he may be a little frightened when you bring
him home, so make sure he feels safe and secure, and provide plenty
of human company until he has adjusted to his new surroundings.*

WHERE TO SLEEP?

You can provide your new kitten with a bed, but if he decides he would prefer to sleep elsewhere, there is little you can do about it. Accept it, and make his chosen bed as comfortable as you can.

It is important that you use a carrier to transport your new kitten home as he could easily become frightened by road traffic. Don't try to carry him in your arms—he could either claw his way out and run away or, if you are in the car, he may inadvertently interfere with the brakes or gas pedal. If a carrier is not provided, you can usually buy an inexpensive cardboard one from a veterinarian or pet shop.

SETTLING IN

When you arrive home with your kitten, confine him to a room (your bedroom will do) along with a litter pan and food and water dishes. It's not a good idea to shut him away by himself. Kittens will miss their siblings and cry all night if left alone. Even if you want an indoor/outdoor cat, you should never put a kitten outdoors until he is ready.

Always leave a litter pan in the room as you can't expect him to be brave enough to explore the new and strange house for the first few days. Sometimes he will be far too frightened even to use the litter pan, and may cling to the security of your bed and wet the bedclothes. This is normal behavior and he will soon remember the purpose of the litter pan.

PLAYING

Your kitten will need a lot of love and attention, and since he no longer has siblings to play with, he will turn to you. In effect, you will become his sibling and he will wrestle your hand, kick and gently nibble you. This is normal behavior and the way in which he burns off excess energy. If his bites become firmer, discourage him by saying "No!" firmly or by blowing softly into his face. Don't pull your hand away too quickly as he may clamp down even harder.

Until he is used to you, don't thrust your hand in his face as you might with a puppy. Hands are large objects and may frighten him. Always talk softly—baby talk is very effective—and move slowly. Gentle petting and grooming are called for, and rough-housing with him should be done carefully.

MEETING OTHER PETS

Don't turn your new kitten loose with your other pets as soon as he arrives home. His most important needs are to feel secure, eat normally and use his litter pan. When ready, one way to introduce him to other cats and dogs is to put a screen door at the entrance to his room so they can meet each other without being able to fight. Another method is to set up a temporary cage in a room where other pets can sniff noses with him but cannot have any spats.

If you don't wish to try these methods, then turn him loose in the house after he has had a few days to settle in. See how the other animals accept him. It is normal to have them hissing and spitting at him. A kitten will not fight, and he is used to his own mother hissing at him and even kicking him away when she has decided he no longer needs to nurse. Your kitten will simply do an about face and walk away.

THE CHAPERONE

Always supervise your pets when they are meeting each other for the first time, and before you leave them on their own be certain that they will not harm each other.

TIME TO PLAY

Although you can give your kitten some toys to play with, what he really wants to play with is you. While he is adjusting to his new home, and to life without his mother and siblings, try to spend as much time with him as possible.

BRINGING YOUR ADULT CAT HOME

If you are adopting an adult cat, you should be aware that it will take time for him to feel secure in his new environment. Be patient as he will come around eventually and you can reap the rewards of having an adult cat, and you will have bypassed most of the training.

If you have acquired an adult cat, transport him home in a carrier, where he will be safe and secure. Don't be tempted to let him loose in the car. He will most likely be fearful and could scratch or bite you while he is trying to hide.

Once home, don't turn him loose in the house. Your primary concern is to ensure that he has a safe refuge away from people and other pets. Unlike a kitten, he will not cry for his siblings, but he will probably seek out a hiding place in his room.

Provide him with water and food dishes and a litter pan in his room. If he hides under a piece of furniture, place a cat bed or small blanket there for his comfort. He will not use a pillow or cat bed in the open until he feels secure. Cats don't like change. They especially dislike moving to a new house or being confronted with any new furniture in their old one. So your adult cat has a double burden to contend with because he has lost both his old home and his old furnishings.

THE NEW HOME

There is no yardstick by which you can measure how long it will take for your cat to feel comfortable. Some will come around within a few days and others may take weeks or even months. Patience is the key to helping him adjust.

Avoid talking loudly and don't make sudden movements. Cats dislike noise and raised voices almost as much as they dislike a new house. Don't pick him up against his will and don't force him to come out of hiding. This will frighten him and he may not be able to trust you again.

As long as he is eating food, drinking water and using his litter pan, you have won half the battle. If he is too afraid to come to you, try sitting quietly on the floor and talking softly to him. On floor level, you no longer appear to be a giant and he is more likely to approach you. Drag a piece of ribbon or string slowly in front of his hiding place and he may creep out. Most important, let him

THE GRAND ENTRANCE
Once home, place your cat safely in a room away from any other pets. He will, in his own time, investigate his new surroundings.

come to you. A sudden move to scoop him up will only send him back into hiding.

Until he feels secure enough to move about his room without fleeing when you enter it, you should not give him access to the rest of the house. But as soon as he does feel at home in the room and with you, open the door and let him explore on his own.

MEETING OTHER PETS
If you have other cats or dogs, it's not a good idea to turn your new cat loose with them. Either keep your cat in a different room while he learns about his new home, or try setting up a large cage in one of the rooms and placing him in it. The cage should be set against a wall so that he can retreat to a safe position when his new friends come to make his acquaintance. You can expect some hissing, growling and raised hair on both sides. This is normal so don't worry. After all, this stranger has invaded the property of your other pets so such reactions are only natural.

After the noises and fluffed tails have subsided, either within a day or two or some weeks, open the door to the cage and let him out, but only

with you standing guard. Don't ever leave him unprotected while you are away from home until you are absolutely certain that all your pets are mixing well together.

You might find that your own cat, who was the leader of the pack, makes a sudden shift in the pecking order and allows the newcomer or one of your other cats to lead the pack. You might also find that your other pets react to this intrusion by developing bad habits of their own. They may be more forceful in their play, use the carpet for a litter pan or even mark their territory by spraying. Neutered males and spayed females are both capable of spraying when provoked (see p. 72).

SNIFFING OUT HOUSEMATES
Make sure your cat has adapted to his new surroundings before introducing him to any other pets.

FOREVER AFTER
Once your adult cat has adjusted to his new home, he will provide you with years of pleasure and companionship.

An Indoor or an Outdoor Cat?

You will need to consider the type of companionship you want from your cat and where you live and your lifestyle before deciding whether yours should be an indoor or an outdoor cat.

OUTSIDE IN

It's never too late to make your cat a totally indoor cat. Just bring him inside and, over only a short period of time, most cats will adapt to their new life in the home.

As a responsible pet owner, you should decide whether you will let your new cat outdoors before you introduce him into your home. If you live close to busy streets, it is best to keep your cat strictly indoors for his own safety. However, if you have a reasonably large yard or live on a farm, you may prefer to allow the cat the freedom to wander indoors or outdoors, as he chooses. The choice is yours, but there are certain points to consider before making the decision.

COMPANIONSHIP

If your cat is kept strictly indoors, you can place a carpeted shelf on a windowsill and open the window to give him the benefit of fresh air and sunshine through the safety of a screen. And he can chatter at the birds as they flit by without harming them.

Many indoor/outdoor cats are loving companions, although for their own protection, they must retain many of the wild instincts necessary for survival. Be aware that your indoor/outdoor cat may bring some of these instincts home. Even if he is neutered, he may still mark his territory every time he enters the house.

He does this by spraying against a door, a piece of furniture or even your bed. Outdoor females, whether

DOMESTIC BLISS

Unlike an outdoor cat, many indoor cats appear to lose their wild instincts and become loving and loyal companions. Some, however, still hunt if they have access to indoor prey.

22

intact or spayed, may also engage in this behavior and, occasionally, the totally indoor cat may as well.

OUTDOOR LIFE

If you have an enclosed yard, your cat may enjoy spending time outside, but keep in mind that he is not totally safe as he can easily wander out of the yard and other cats can wander in.

The dangers your cat may encounter outdoors range from being attacked by neighboring cats or dogs to being struck by an automobile. An abscess can result from a cat or dog bite, but it may not be visible until the infection has spread via his bloodstream through much of his body.

FARM LIFE

If yours is a working cat on a farm or ranch, he will have to learn to avoid the dangers of livestock and moving vehicles on his own as there is little you can do to help him. Make sure that you keep his vaccinations current and ensure that he has a dry, comfortable place to sleep.

Check with your vet as to what flea preventives are recommended, such as a monthly oral dose or topical treatments. If these are not available, a flea collar may help a little, as will dustings of flea powder on both his body and his bedding.

UNALTERED CATS

If your cat is unaltered and goes outdoors, you will need to check him frequently for wounds inflicted by other tomcats. If females have

kittens, they should be provided with a secure retreat to protect the young from predators—even their own father may be a threat.

So if you have an outdoor cat, you should ensure that he is neutered. This will also help to reduce the number of unwanted kittens that are born every year, many of which become feral and pose a threat to wildlife.

PERILS OF OUTDOOR LIFE
An outdoor cat is at risk of flea and worm infestation. You will be fighting a losing battle trying to rid your house of fleas as well, because he will reinfest your home each time he returns.

SAFEGUARDING YOUR TREASURES

Most cats are not destructive, we only think they are. If he knocks a figurine off a shelf, it is nothing more than playtime for him, but a severe loss to us if it is a priceless heirloom. To safeguard your treasures, try attaching them to the surfaces. Generally, such things as the table lamp and the curios are kept in the same locations, so fastening them won't ruin your decor, and there are adhesives now available that won't damage the finish on your tables or shelving.

Your cat may engage in unacceptable behavior if you change his routine or leave him alone for a period of time he considers too long. He may ignore you or go about the house unrolling the toilet paper, knocking magazines and knickknacks off every surface, and generally rearranging anything movable if he is really mad at you.

SPAYING AND NEUTERING

Unless you are a breeder, your cat will be far happier and make a better pet if he is neutered. This will also help reduce the number of unwanted cats, and may save you a considerable sum of money in medical costs.

If left unaltered, your male cat may howl, pace about and saturate your drapes and furniture with urine. If you have a female cat, be aware that she can come into season as often as every few weeks throughout some parts of the year. She, too, may howl, pace and ruin your furnishings by spraying. If this sounds unappealing, you may want to consider spaying or neutering your cat.

SPAYING

Some females may lose weight when they are in season and may not have time to regain the weight before having another season. A female cat who has had even one litter of kittens may run a greater chance of contracting breast cancer than does the female who has been spayed without ever going through a heat. If you have a female who is not spayed, she can be susceptible to pyometra (a uterine infection) because of frequent seasons. Pyometra (see p. 64) can be fatal if not detected and treated in time.

To reduce the incidence of disease and infection, the best thing to do is spay your female cat. Spaying a cat (removing her uterus and ovaries) is a routine operation and usually requires no more than an overnight stay at the veterinary clinic. The procedure is simple and your cat will fully recover in a few days.

NEUTERING

Although some people have no qualms about having a female spayed as they do not want her to have kittens, they may balk at having a male neutered. If you let him outdoors, however, you may be responsible for contributing to the number of unwanted cats and kittens that are destroyed each year by humane societies. Neutering a male cat (removing the testicles) is a simple procedure and could avoid problems an unaltered cat may experience.

Intact males are more susceptible to diseases such as feline immunodeficiency

FOR THE BEST
Your veterinarian will advise you on the best age to have your cat neutered. Although kittens can be spayed or neutered as early as eight weeks, many veterinarians recommend waiting until the kitten is about six months old.

AT THE VETERINARIAN
When a female kitten is spayed, the veterinarian will remove her uterus and ovaries. This is a more involved operation than neutering a male (removing the testicles) and it will take her a few days to recover fully.

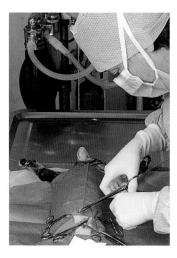

Many humane shelters will not release a kitten or cat for adoption unless he or she is first neutered or spayed. And, because of the large number of unwanted kittens, some shelters have been neutering or spaying kittens as young as eight weeks of age. However, if you are acquiring your kitten from a breeder, seek advice from your veterinarian.

FINANCIAL CONSIDERATIONS

Spaying or neutering costs should be considered when deciding to add a cat to your household. The cost of altering a cat varies from place to place. The fees may seem expensive, but they pale in comparison with the potential fees involved with treating an unaltered male for wounds that result from fighting with other tomcats if you let him outdoors. They are also less expensive than replacing your carpet or furniture because of spraying.

Most vets set their fees at a price most cat owners can afford. If you are on a limited income and cannot afford the full price, contact your town authorities and local veterinarians to locate a low-cost neutering program.

virus (FIV), passed on in close contact, and to injuries acquired in fights with other cats or by being hit by cars while searching for females.

The myth that an altered cat will become grossly overweight and no longer be a playful companion is not true. Because of the decreased activity associated with neutering, he may not require as much food or may require food with a lower fat content. Very often, he will revert to his kittenish self and become even more playful, since he will not be distracted by the mating urge. He will tend to give you much more affection than previously. Also, there is no truth to the myth that a neutered male is more susceptible to urinary tract disease (see p. 64).

neutered or spayed from about eight weeks of age. Many veterinarians, however, are most comfortable with performing these procedures on older cats, when they are about six months old. Factors that may affect the decision about when to spay and neuter include the cat's size and health status.

Each cat differs as to his development but aside from the obvious signs of fully developed testicles, you will notice that his behavior has changed radically. Overnight, he may go from a frisky kitten to an aggressive male who plays too roughly with you and the other cats. If this happens, it is a clear sign that it is time to have him neutered.

AT WHAT AGE?
You should follow the advice of your veterinarian about when to have your cat spayed or neutered. Kittens of both sexes can be

THE STUD
Unless, as with this Oriental, you are planning to use your cat for breeding purposes, it is important to have him neutered.

RESPONSIBLE CAT OWNERSHIP

Before acquiring or selling a cat, there are a number of practical and legal issues you should consider. Possibly the most important is to ensure that he is both registered and fitted with clear identification.

If you have a pedigreed cat, you should have been given his papers when you acquired him. These consist of a registration certificate or application for registration completed by the breeder as well as a pedigree showing his family tree.

If you have a mixed-breed cat, it's still a good idea to register him. Almost all of the cat-registering associations offer registration in the household pet category. Their only condition is that any cat so registered not be used for breeding—a requirement aimed at reducing the number of unwanted kittens. As well as the major associations, there

are a number of independent groups that register mixed breeds. These can be located through ads in cat magazines.

In some states in the U.S., cats are considered feral and, as such, have no rights under the relevant state's laws. Although rarely enforced, you should make inquiries to be certain of your cat's status.

ADVANTAGES
The advantages of having a registration certificate on your cat are many. First, it identifies him as to sex, color,

IDENTIFICATION

If your cat ventures outdoors, there is a huge variety of tags available to attach to his collar for identification purposes. The break-away collar is recommended for safety, however, if the collar does break away, he will lose his identifications. Another alternative is to have your veterinarian implant a microchip under his skin. This will identify him to any veterinarian or animal shelter with the appropriate scanning device.

CHOOSING A PEDIGREE

When purchasing pedigreed cats, such as these Chartreux, details of a minimum of three generations should be supplied. If you plan to show, a minimum of five generations is now considered mandatory.

eye color, hair length and age. In the case of the purebred, it registers his breed as well. If he goes outdoors and is picked up by another person, it will help identify him as your cat. If you have multiple cats and meet with an accident, it will serve to identify your cats and make their placement easier.

In an extreme case, if your cat wreaks havoc in a neighbor's garden, and that neighbor then harms him, the certificate will serve as proof of ownership in the event that you take the neighbor to court for damages.

THE SHELTER

If you acquire a cat from the shelter, or rescue center, you will be bound by their rules, and most will require that any animal leaving their kennel be neutered or spayed, regardless of age. In the U.S., veterinarians are now neutering and spaying kittens as early as eight weeks of age. However, in Britain, this is not commonly done until cats are six months old.

BREEDER OR PET STORE

If you buy a cat from a breeder or a pet store, ask about a health guarantee. The ethical person will give you a certain number of days during which you should have the cat examined by your veterinarian. If he is not healthy, you may be able to return him and receive a full refund.

SELLING YOUR KITTEN

Before a kitten is sold, he should have received at least his first vaccination and instructions should be given as to when others are due. If selling him at a pet price—not for breeding or showing—you don't need papers. Often, though, papers will be given upon proof from a veterinarian that the cat has been neutered or spayed. At other times, breeders will issue the papers and check the space to indicate the kitten is still to be neutered or spayed.

If you are selling him as a breeder or show cat, then he will command a higher price and you are bound to provide his papers as well. There is no reason why you shouldn't have all documents ready, so a buyer should never accept him unless all relevant papers are available at the time of sale.

UNFORESEEN EVENTS

Make provisions for your cat in case of your unexpected hospitalization or death. Any animals confined in the house may suffer from neglect, so be sure to leave written word with a friend, relative or neighbor so they can gain entry and take care of your pets should the need arise.

FOR SALE
You should always take your new kitten or cat to a veterinarian for a checkup, regardless of where you acquired him. He should be in good health and free from any parasites. However, if you have had him for more than ten days, and he comes down with a cold or something similarly minor, don't worry as this is to be expected and is no cause for concern.

QUARANTINED
If you are moving to another country, your cat may need to be quarantined. Check with the relevant authorities about the quarantine laws in that country.

CARING FOR YOUR CAT

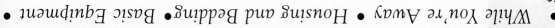

See the kitten on the wall
Sporting with the leaves that fall,
Withered leaves—one, two and three
From the lofty elder-tree!

WILLIAM WORDSWORTH (1770-1850),
English poet

HOUSING AND BEDDING

*It is important to provide a safe and comfortable home for
your cat. You should take precautions to reduce the number
of accidents that could occur in your home, and you must be
sure she has her own haven in which to rest.*

SAFETY IN THE HOUSE
Even though your cat may now
be a mature adult, you will still
need to ensure that the home is
as safe as possible—just as you
would for a child.

AMONG THE COVERS
Although you can provide your
new kitten with a comfortable bed,
there is no guarantee that she will
use it. In fact, she may well prefer
to sleep on your bed.

It's impossible to
ensure that your
house is totally safe
for your cat. Think
of her as a toddler
and take the same
precautions you would
with a child. Keep all
medicines in a locked
cabinet, and keep all your
household cleaning agents
safely behind a locked or
latched door. When running
water into the bathtub, keep
the door closed so that she
won't fall in. If fully grown,
all that will be hurt will be
her dignity. If she is a kitten,
she may slip and drown.
Always keep the toilet lid
closed for the same reasons.

Be especially careful when
opening the oven door as the
aromas of food baking may
attract her to jump in. While
cooking on the stove, either
keep her out of the kitchen or
watch her closely. Again, the
enticing aromas of food may
beckon her to jump onto the
stove. Not only can she suffer
burns on her feet from a
burner still radiating heat, but
her tail trailing across a lit
burner can singe her hair. Or
her face peering nosily into a
pan can singe her whiskers.

Your cat will also be
attracted to your washer and
dryer as they offer excellent
sources of warmth to her. She
can be very quick and you
may think she is safely
sleeping elsewhere, but when
you close the door to the
dryer, she may have already
jumped into it. Always check
these appliances to make sure
they are cat-free before
turning them on.

If you have a fireplace,
make sure that it is tightly
screened or that the screen
can be fastened securely with
hooks. Cats don't seem to fear
fire as they should and she
may try to lie down next to a
burning log if not kept out.

Before opening any windows,
make sure that the screens are
securely fastened. A fall to the
pavement can be fatal as cats
don't always land on their
feet, especially if the tumble is

WARM AND DRY

Always keep the door to both your washer and dryer closed. Your cat may seek out its warmth, and you could turn it on without her having a chance to escape.

bean bag

unexpected. When opening outside doors, or even internal ones if there is a cross-breeze, use a doorstop. Many a cat has lost part of her tail by having a door slam shut on it.

A SAFE PLACE TO SLEEP
You can make a comfortable sleeping place for your cat by placing a ring pillow—a round, stuffed pillow, with sides about 4 inches (10 cm) high—on a piece of furniture, preferably against a wall. She wants the security of being above floor level and with a solid wall at her back. If she has a short or a fine coat and needs extra warmth, place a lamp with a low wattage bulb near the pillow. Make sure it is securely fastened so it can't tip over, and hide the cord so the cat won't chew on it.

If you are not adverse to having her in the kitchen, a pillow on top of the refrigerator or the washer or dryer makes a good comfort station. Again, she is up high, and the heat from these appliances will keep her warm.

She may decide that an upholstered chair or your bed is her cup of tea, so provide her with a pillow or small blanket for those areas. Or she may prefer to sleep under your bed covers. She will let you know where she wants to sleep and you can outfit

her favorite spot with a comfortable towel or pillow.

Another location that makes her feel safe is the floor of the closet with the door left slightly ajar. She won't feel threatened there as it is dark and quiet. A pillow or other bedding on the floor of the closet may suit her very well. Or you might consider giving her a shelf in a closet. Again, you should place comfortable bedding on the shelf. Your cat will need her own place of refuge as cats do a lot of sleeping and need a safe place in which they can fully relax and not be on guard against children or other household pets.

cat sock

wicker basket

ring pillow

BASIC EQUIPMENT

Before you bring your new cat home, make sure you have purchased
all the necessary equipment. Today there is a greater choice of
products on the market than ever before, so choose wisely,
and to begin with, buy only what you really need.

recycled paper litter

litter made from rice husks

diatomite

shredded newspaper

The items that you should consider before bringing your cat home are litter, litter pan, bowls and saucers, scratching post or pad, collar, grooming equipment, cat flap, bedding, toys, cage and carrying case.

LITTER

The type of litter you choose for your cat depends entirely on how much you want to spend and how fussy you are about sand, clay, wood shavings and such being tracked through your house.

An economical material for litter is newspaper. Simply line the pan with a section from the newspaper and then cover with strips torn from another section. After the cat uses the litter pan, it is easy to roll up the entire newspaper and dispose of it. This avoids unsightly litter being tracked throughout your house, and it also minimizes odor as the urine is removed from the house, along with her bowel movements. When using a scoop to remove solids from normal litter or clay, too often the urine-soaked litter remains for days at a time. This not only results in an offensive odor that will soon permeate your house but your cat very often will not want to use the litter pan. Cats do not like to be dirty or have wet feet. If the pan has wet litter in it, she may well decide that a corner of the carpet or your bedspread make perfectly fine—and dry—litter pans.

After you have disposed of the contents of the pan (the frequency will depend on the number of cats using it and the odor), make sure that you thoroughly clean the inside and outside of it, using a non-toxic cleaner. If you use a strong cleaning agent, make sure that you rinse the pan completely so that no residual effects of the cleaner can harm her.

LITTER PAN

The size of your cat's litter pan depends on how large she is and if she will be sharing it

litter pan

poop scoop

plastic double-feeder

plastic bowl

plastic saucer

metal food bowl

metal water dish

ceramic dish

scratching post

with any other cats. You can purchase a plastic litter pan at any grocery or pet store. And it's a good idea to have a few disposable cardboard pans on hand. These are useful for short trips with your cat. Or if you have a friend coming by to take care of her while you are gone, it makes it easier for your friend if the entire litter pan, contents and all, can be thrown out.

Litter pans also come with hoods or are completely enclosed with just a small opening for your cat to enter. The problem with this type of litter pan is that she will very often splash urine against the sides of the enclosure making even more work for you in cleaning not only the pan, but the enclosure as well.

BOWLS AND SAUCERS

Your cat will need bowls for both water and dry food. She will also need a flat saucer for moist or wet food (see p. 47). If there are other cats in the house, or if you are feeding outdoor cats, a water feeder and a dispenser for dry food are excellent (see p. 50). These can hold a larger amount of water and food than bowls, and have protective covers to keep the contents fresher and free from dirt and dust.

A water feeder is also useful if you are away from home for several hours at a time, because it means your cat will not go thirsty if she knocks it over.

SCRATCHING POSTS AND PADS

A scratching post or pad (a post that rests on the floor) is one of the essential items you need to purchase if your cat is to remain indoors unless, of course, you want your cat to scratch the furniture. An indoor/outdoor cat, on the other hand, will simply use the trunk of a tree. Because she likes a good full stretch when scratching, the post should be taller than she is when stretching her body to full length and raising her front legs. A tightly woven carpeted post is preferable to a loosely woven one, and a good choice is indoor/outdoor carpet. Another favorite is a sturdy log or orange crate. Or you can purchase or make a post or pad with sisal rope. Simply wrap the sisal tightly around a length of wood. This can be either free-standing or nailed to a door frame.

COLLARS, LEASHES AND HARNESSES

If your cat is always indoors, she will not need a collar. If you want her to wear one for decorative purposes, or in case she slips outside and is found, or if she is an indoor/outdoor cat, then make sure the collar has the break-away feature to keep her from being strangled if it becomes snagged.

A leash is needed only if you want to train your cat to take walks with you. The leash should be of a light material and, given that your adult cat may range from 5 to 25 lb (2 to 11 kg), it should be suitable for her size. It should never be fastened to any collar. Only a figure-8 harness, made expressly for cats, should be used with the leash. A dog harness is not suitable and a collar is too easy for her to slip out of and she might run away.

leash

figure-8 harness

assorted collars

GROOMING EQUIPMENT

Your cat will need her own combs and brushes. The types you buy will depend on whether she has a short or long coat and fine or thick hair. Cotton swabs for ear-cleaning are also a must, as well as scissors made especially for trimming claws (see pp. 36–43).

CAT FLAPS

If she is allowed outside, a cat flap makes an excellent door for your cat. These range from models that can be fitted to a screen door to solid wooden ones. Some cat flaps can be opened only by an electronic chip on her collar that opens the door as she approaches. This is a good choice if she is the type of cat that invites other cats home for lunch. It also serves to stop any potential predators, such as small dogs or wildlife, from entering.

BEDS AND BASKETS

Since cats spend so much time sleeping, it's important to provide them with a bed. It should be big enough for her to stretch out in when she is fully grown, and enclosed on at least three sides for cosiness and a sense of security.

Baskets and beds come in wicker, plastic or fiberglass. Or you can make yourself one by lining a cardboard box with sides high enough to exclude drafts. A soft blanket or pillow placed inside is ideal.

A popular bed is a bean bag which is filled with polystyrene and covered with a removable washable material. Another favorite is a ring, or donut, pillow (see p. 31).

TOYS

There are many cat toys on the market. Although the best ones have you attached, your cat will need toys for when you're away or too busy to play with her.

You can either make your own toys (see p. 45) or purchase them. The stores are full of toys for cats but make

enclosed carrying case

wire-top carrying case

sure that any you purchase are free of small attachments. These can come off easily and be accidentally swallowed. A good rule of thumb is to ask yourself if the toy is safe for a human baby. If not, then it is probably not safe for your cat.

CAGES

A cage to confine your cat is a good idea if you have guests who are not fond of cats on their laps or if your cat is ill and needs to be kept in one place. A large kennel will do. Or you could adapt your child's playpen or crib by placing a lid on it. In the case of the crib, cover the sides with hardware cloth, or wire.

CARRYING CASES

A carrying case is an essential piece of equipment. They can range from inexpensive cardboard types to designer cases. Your cat should be confined to a case when traveling by car, train or airplane, and should always be taken to the veterinarian in one.

A cat is not safe in the veterinarian's examining room on your lap or on a leash. Even if other animals present in the waiting room cannot actually reach her to harm her, she may think they can, and this can add needless stress and anxiety to your cat, who may already feel ill.

assorted balls

assorted toy mice

GROOMING

All cat owners will need to spend at least some time grooming their cat. However the length of time you choose to spend will depend on whether she is an indoor or outdoor cat, whether she is longhaired or shorthaired, and whether you plan to show her or just have her as a companion.

EXTRA CLEANING
All cats clean themselves regularly. However, if you are intending to show your cat, you will need to wash her thoroughly to properly prepare her coat.

A cat is one of the cleanest creatures on earth, and spends a large part of her waking hours washing herself. She can go through life very nicely without ever having a bath, as regular combing and brushing will suffice. But if you are a cat fancier and plan on showing her, then you must always present her in tip-top shape, and groom and wash her regularly. She will also need a bath if she has a foreign or toxic substance on her coat that must be washed off immediately. Or you may need to remove soot if she has been playing in the fireplace. Or if she is an indoor/outdoor cat, she may have an accumulation of household dust or dirt that needs to be washed off.

Your cat's saliva could either turn your cat's dark coat a reddish color, or her white or light-colored coat a yellowish color. Sunlight may also affect the color of her coat. So no matter how many times you wash her, you may never be able to keep her coat completely stain-free.

CLEANING HER EARS
Either before or after her bath, you may clean her ears by dipping a cotton swab into mineral oil or boric-acid powder. Remove the dirt and

EAR-CLEANING
Only clean the visible part of your cat's ears. Never put the swab into her ear canal as it can cause damage.

FACE-CLEANING
To prevent tear and saliva staining, you may need to clean your cat's face on a regular basis.

TRIMMING CLAWS

If you start trimming your cat's claws when she is a kitten, she will discover that it doesn't hurt one bit and will resign herself to the process. It's probably best to trim her claws before you bathe her.

By squeezing her toe between your forefinger and thumb, her claw will be easily extended and can be trimmed with special clippers made for cats. Be sure to avoid the sensitive pink quick and to remove only the very tip. Hold her gently and talk softly while clipping. Don't panic and don't raise your voice. A loud, angry or high-pitched voice only makes her more anxious and fearful. She won't mind you clipping the front claws, but when you turn her over on her back, she may try to fight you. Do not tighten your hold. Pause for a moment, continue to talk quietly and you might even try blowing softly into her face, at the same time saying "no" in a low but firm voice. Do not let her free until you have completed trimming all of her claws.

If she is a kitten, she will need her claws clipped once a week, but when she is fully grown, every two weeks will suffice.

EXTEND CLAWS
Firmly but gently place the cat in your lap, and then press down on the pad to extend the claw.

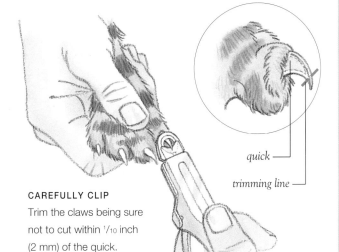

quick —
trimming line —

CAREFULLY CLIP
Trim the claws being sure not to cut within 1/10 inch (2 mm) of the quick.

any excess wax from inside the ear flap. Never probe down into the ear canal.

CLEANING HER FACE
The rest of her face can be cleaned with a soft cloth dipped in warm water. You might even make this part of a daily routine to freshen her face and remove any eye matter that usually accumulates in the corners of her eyes.

Some cats, especially those with flatter faces such as the Persian, develop tear track stains on their faces. To remove, prepare a paste of either cornstarch or boric acid mixed with enough peroxide to form the paste. Be especially careful when working anywhere near her eyes. Apply the mixture to the stained area with a cotton swab or cotton ball.

Although tear tracks should be washed off regularly, you will only need to use the mixture every few times. Water will suffice on the other occasions. If not washed daily, she could develop deep furrows that can actually fester simply from the continuous moisture of tears against her skin.

SCISSOR OR GUILLOTINE
When trimming claws, you can either use scissor-action or guillotine-action clippers.

WET BATHS

It is best to start giving wet baths to your cat while she is still a kitten and is small enough to be held easily. It is also best to attempt to give her a bath by yourself. Another pair of hands can panic her and increase her struggle to free herself. The ideal spot for her bath is any sizable sink or bowl that is about waist-high to you. The height most comfortable is that of the kitchen sink. Cats are easily frightened if you place them in a low-lying basin and loom over them. It is also more difficult for you to hold them and control them in that awkward position.

Have all of your shampoos, rinses or flea-dip preparations ready, as well as a soft towel for washing her face and a large towel for the initial drying of her coat. Make sure they are placed within easy reach of you but out of reach of your cat. Initially, she will attempt to attach herself to anything in close range in order to escape the water.

The choice of shampoos is up to you and depends upon her coat type. A shampoo containing a whitener is recommended for white cats, or if she has a skin or flea problem, you should use a chemical flea shampoo. You may also use a mild human shampoo, such as one you would use for babies, and finish off with any good-quality conditioner.

Don't worry about washing inside her ears as this is best done separately. Some experts advise putting a cotton ball inside her ears so that water will not penetrate. This is not a good idea as it could alarm her. Others say to put petroleum jelly around her eyes so that shampoo will not enter. This, too, is bad advice as it will not fully prevent the suds from getting into her eyes. The jelly will bother her to the extent that she will keep trying to wipe it off and so interfere with your being able to bathe her. She will probably spread it through her coat as well.

Place a rubber mat or towel in the bottom of the sink. Fill it with lukewarm water that comes up to her shoulders. Place her in the water facing away from you. Never let her face you as she can stretch her

STARTING YOUNG
If you are planning to bathe your cat regularly, you should start when she is still a kitten. Like this Bengal, she will quickly become accustomed to the process, and not struggle when she is older.

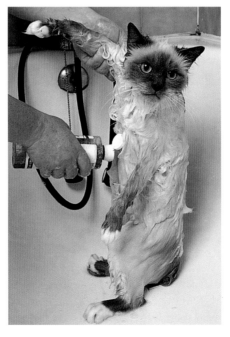

THE BATH
Unless, like this Birman, your cat is comfortable with being given a bath, never have her facing toward you as she can easily reach out to scratch you.

legs out much farther than you expect and claw into your clothing or arms.

If you place all four of her feet into the water at once, she will generally settle down. Then put one hand across her shoulders, very gently (she will struggle mightily if the pressure is too great), and use the other hand to wet her down and apply the shampoo. Avoid grasping the back of her neck. Although this will calm down a kitten as she is accustomed to her mother subduing her in that fashion, the adult cat will only struggle more.

Move slowly and talk softly. It is not necessary to apply shampoo directly onto her face as you can more safely wash her ears and face with the cloth dipped into the bath water at another time.

After you have lathered her, rinse the shampoo off with either glassfuls of water or a rubber spray hose. Be sure to rinse all of the shampoo out of her coat as even a small amount left will cause her to froth at the mouth when she starts licking herself after the bath. If a conditioner is used, make sure to thoroughly rinse it off in the same manner. Then gather her up in the towel, wrap it around her securely, and carry her to a

AFTER THE BATH
Wrap your cat in a towel as soon as you have finished washing her. This will not only soak up the excess moisture, but will help her to relax.

draft-free room. She may tremble from fear or anxiety, so sit down with her and let the towel absorb the excess moisture while you speak reassuringly to her.

DRY BATHS
If you don't feel up to giving her a wet bath, if she has an infection, or if the weather is cold, then it's probably best to give your cat a dry bath. There are a number of dry shampoo products on the market. Sprinkle the powder through her coat and brush it off. Use a towel to remove any excess powder. Cats hate anything foreign on their coat, and the powder may irritate her.

dry shampoo

fine-toothed comb

brush

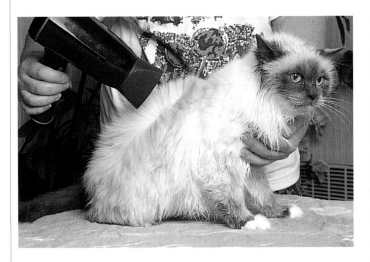

calls for a sleek coat lying flat, then the dryer would add too much fullness for her to have much success.

DRYING LONGHAIRED OR MEDIUM-HAIRED CATS

If yours is a longhaired or medium-haired cat, you will have extra work to do as self-drying is not really suitable for her. As she dries, you must continually comb through her coat so that it does not tangle. If you start this process when she is young, you can quickly accustom her to the hair dryer, which will dramatically speed up the process.

Whether drying your cat's coat naturally or with the assistance of a hair dryer, you should continue to comb her coat until it is completely dry. If she won't hold still enough for you to comb her with one hand and hold the dryer with the other hand, you will need some assistance. Try to construct a makeshift holder for the hair dryer or purchase an inexpensive dryer and stand from the pet store.

A QUICKER APPROACH
A hair dryer will definitely speed up the drying process, particularly if you have a Birman or other longhaired cat.

DRYING SHORTHAIRED CATS

If it is a warm day, and if she is a shorthaired cat, let her dry naturally in a room. However, you should make sure all windows remain closed until she is completely dry. Any draft, even a warm one, can be harmful to her.

If it is a cool day you can turn on an electric heater to speed up the process. You could attempt to dry her with a hair dryer if she is a shorthaired companion cat. However, if she is a show cat whose standard

plastic flea combs

blunt-tipped scissors

grooming glove for longhaired cats

brush for detangling matted hair

GROOMING SHORTHAIRED CATS

Accustom your shorthaired cat to combing every three or four days as soon as you acquire her. Use a comb with small, close teeth. Start combing at the back of her neck and work your way down to her tail, following the fall of her hair. Be especially careful around her hindquarters and other such sensitive areas. Then repeat the combing using a hard rubber brush.

The natural oils as found on the palms of your hands are great for making her coat lie flat. Daily petting by you can be just about as effective as brushing her.

If you'd like, finish off her shorthaired coat by running a chamois or silk scarf over it.

If your cat has a sore that requires medication, ask your veterinarian about a dry powder instead of an ointment. Your cat will hate the feel of ointment and do her best to lick it off. A powder, though, shouldn't bother her and may hasten the drying process of the sore enabling it to heal more quickly.

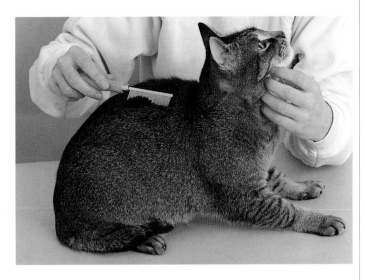

INITIAL COMBING

Use a fine-toothed metal comb for the initial combing of your cat. Be sure to keep a close watch for any sign of fleas or parasites.

ANOTHER COMB

Repeat the process using a hard rubber brush. This will enable you to apply more pressure without causing your cat any discomfort.

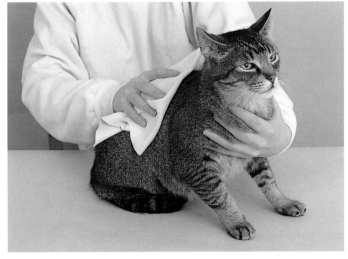

FINISHING OFF

After combing and brushing your cat, rub the palm of your hand over her coat, and then give her a final wipe with a chamois.

41

POWDERING UP
Before you start combing your longhaired cat, sprinkle cornstarch or fuller's earth through her coat and then massage it in to ensure the powder is evenly spread.

GROOMING LONGHAIRED CATS

If you have a longhaired cat, then you have your work cut out for you, and if you plan to show her, you will need to put in extra effort. Aside from the length of time required to comb her as she dries after a bath, you can expect to be her personal scrub nurse every day. She may not be able to avoid clumps of fecal matter on her coat no matter how hard she tries. The very fact that she has long hair around her rear end and the britches (the back of her legs) makes it almost impossible for her to avoid becoming messy.

You will need to regularly inspect your cat's rear end to see if she is clean. If not, stand her on a bench with her rear end hanging over a basin, and wash the stained area with warm water and a mild soap, being sure to rinse it thoroughly. If she has just a small amount clinging to her britches, you can pluck it off and then powder her—with cornstarch if she is a light-colored cat or fuller's earth if she is dark-colored cat—as you comb through the hair.

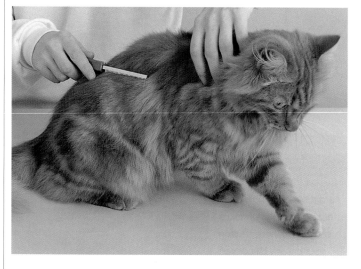

DETANGLING
Using a wide-toothed comb, comb out any knots or tangles in her coat. If the tangles are extensive, you may need to use scissors to cut them out.

If she is one of the tailless breeds—such as the Manx, Cymric or Japanese Bobtail—she may have the same problem, even if she is short-haired. She may lack the ability to sever the feces neatly and cleanly and it will very often attach itself to her legs. Since she has no tail, you can easily see if she needs attention and clean her up as prescribed for the longhaired cat.

To make it easier to groom her long hair, sprinkle either

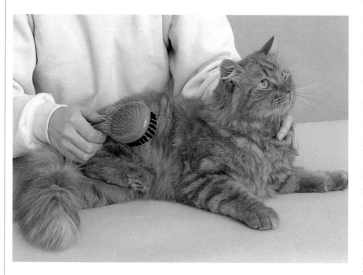

FLUFFING UP
Finally, move a soft brush up and down her body, including her tail and legs. Finish by brushing against the line of the hair for fullness.

cornstarch or fuller's earth through her coat. The powder will loosen the tangles and make it easier for the teeth of the comb to slip through. Use a wide-toothed comb for removing tangles. Pay special attention to her britches, tail and stomach. You can reach her stomach by turning her upside down on your lap. Make this an enjoyable time and combine affection with play (such as dangling your necklace or chain to amuse her).

Even with daily combing, though, her coat may be of such a consistency that she will sweat on her tummy area and mats will form. To remove these, use blunt-tipped scissors. Separate the mat as much as you can with your fingers. Then, place one of your fingers against her skin so that you will not stab her as you cut off the mat.

If for some reason you have not kept up with her daily grooming and she develops severe mats that you are unable to remove, you must seek professional help from a cat groomer or your veterinarian right away. If not taken care of, the mats will twist into such a snarl that they will pinch her skin quite painfully.

You'll need to use a soft brush for her ruff (the hair framing her neck) as this should stand out away from her body. And pay special attention to her toes. Longhaired cats grow toe tufts that are beautiful to see but can tangle just as her body

hair does. Finish off her longhaired coat by brushing or combing her hair the wrong way so that it stands out from her body.

DENTAL AND GUM CARE

Your veterinarian should check your cat's mouth on her yearly physical and will usually clean her teeth. In the meantime, you should regularly check her teeth and gums for soreness, tartar or diseased or broken teeth.

You can help ward off gum infection and tooth decay by cleaning your cat's teeth on a regular basis. It's easiest to do this if you start the practice when she's a kitten as she will quickly become accustomed to it. Begin by wrapping a small bit of gauze around your finger and then gently rubbing on and around the teeth and along the gums. Then you can graduate to an actual cat toothbrush (make sure you use one made expressly for cats) and cat toothpaste.

cat's toothbrush

GUM MASSAGE

Prevention is better than cure. So take the time regularly to massage your cat's gums and teeth to help prevent disease and the buildup of tartar.

WHITE AND BRIGHT

Never use toothpaste made for humans when brushing your cat's teeth. Your veterinarian or local pet store should be able to supply you with some made especially for cats.

EXERCISE REQUIREMENTS

Cats, especially kittens, will generally get all the exercise they need through their everyday activities. However, all cats will enjoy the extra exercise they have when you play with them.

Your new kitten will eat, sleep and, on waking, run about the house like one possessed. She will make her tail bushy and even leap up on the walls, and this behavior will continue from when she is about six weeks old until she settles down as an adult, although she may still act like a kitten well into adulthood.

While she is still a kitten, she will want to play every waking moment. Don't overdo the playtime though, as you can cause her to feel stressed and overtired.

Your kitten will attack her siblings with tooth and claw and you'll wonder how any of them manage to survive kittenhood. Her mother will tolerate the tail-biting and ear-chewing, but will let the kitten know when enough is enough by seizing her baby's neck between her teeth and settling her down. When you acquire her as a single kitten, she will use you as her siblings. Gentle rough-housing is fine, but don't overdo it. Treat her as you would a baby or toddler. Don't swing her up in the air as you might a baby though— keep her at lap level or below.

PLAYTIME

Unlike dogs, your cat will not need to be taken for walks. She will have all the exercise she needs in her everyday activities, but, as with this Burmese, her favorite form of exercise is always the one in which you are involved.

A BAG OF FUN

If you don't have time to play with your cat, a paper bag left on the floor is sure to give her enjoyment as she hides deep inside and then pounces on you as you pass by.

PLAYTIME

The best toy is one with you at the other end. Your cat loves to pounce on your toes or fingers as they move underneath the bedcovers. Anything that dangles is appealing to her. Make sure that toys have no loose strips that the kitten could chew off and swallow. A bit of string, a belt or a ribbon trailed across the floor or in front of her hiding place is sure to elicit a delighted pounce and scamper after the trailing end. Or make a fishing pole from a stick, some fishing line, and a bit of cloth on the end of the line. A ball of aluminum foil is light and rolls well. A pipe cleaner bent in a circle and tossed will result in endless fun for her as she picks it up in her mouth and returns it (or drops it just out of reach, which she thinks is hilarious). Or take a cardboard box, seal it, and cut holes on the top and sides large enough for her to pass through. Toss a toy or two inside for hours of amusement.

VENTURING OUTDOORS

Your indoor cat can always find plenty of exercise in her home, but if you want to take your indoor cat outside for some sunshine and to smell the roses, try to make her adapt to walking on a harness and leash (see p. 34). Don't consider this proper exercise, though, as she will generally curl herself into a clump so that you have to move her along by gently tugging on the leash.

OUTDOOR CATS

If your cat goes outdoors, she will run rapidly after real or imagined prey. To an indoor/outdoor cat, a leaf wafting across the lawn is as attractive as a bird or mouse. As for the working cat, she will develop and retain her muscles and condition by keeping the ranch or farm free of rodents and other vermin. The indoor/outdoor cat, as well as the completely outdoor cat, gets plenty of exercise as she is compelled to make the rounds of her territory every day. She will leave her mark either by spraying, rubbing her cheek against a tree or building, or leaving scars in tree trunks from her claws. This daily patrol not only keeps her busy, but keeps her fit, too.

AGING CATS

As your cat grows older, she may sleep more and more. In addition to watching her diet, you need to encourage her to play by leaving toys out and setting aside time each and every day to spend with her.

A GOOD COMPANION
With a lot of time and patience on your part, the day may come when your cat will trot along quite nicely on a leash and get plenty of exercise.

THE GREAT OUTDOORS
An outdoor cat, such as this Burmese, may get all the exercise she needs chasing leaves, birds and rodents, and patrolling and marking territory.

FEEDING YOUR CAT

Good nutrition is the cornerstone of good health. Equipped with basic knowledge, you will find that providing the best possible nutrition for your cat is neither difficult nor complex.

dry cat food

TO THEIR HEALTH

Good commercial cat foods are complete, balanced and easy to feed. Cats live far longer today than 50 years ago, at least in part because of advances in feline nutrition.

It is essential that cats have access to clean fresh water at all times, regardless of the nature of the diet. Cats are obligate carnivores. This means they must eat meat (including poultry and fish) to satisfy their uniquely high protein requirement, and to obtain essential substances, such as the amino acid taurine, which they are unable to manufacture from non-meat foods. Cats cannot live on meat alone, but require many nutrients that are supplied in proper balance in good commercial cat foods.

CHOOSING FOODS

Manufactured cat foods are safe and wholesome. The U.S. Food and Drug Administration specifies ingredients and processes manufacturers must use and regulates claims on labels. The Association of American Feed Control Officials (AAFCO) sets nutritional-adequacy standards. So, when choosing food, examine labels for this information:
1. "Complete and balanced," means that all essential nutrients are present in proper proportions;
2. A declaration that the product meets AAFCO standards;
3. The life-stage statement indicates the target group for the food: "all life stages" or "adult maintenance;"
4. Animal protein sources, including poultry or fish, will head the list of dry-food ingredients or, in canned food, immediately follow water. Ingredients appear in descending order by weight.

PREMIUM OR NOT?

Cat foods sold in grocery stores may seem less expensive than premium brands, which

HEALTHY KITTENS

Kittens thrive on a balanced diet specifically formulated for their active lives.

are generally available only from pet stores, feed stores or veterinarians. But premium brands usually offer several important advantages. Ounce for ounce, the high-quality ingredients in premium foods deliver more energy, are more completely digested and absorbed, and yield less waste, so can be fed in smaller portions.

CANNED OR DRY?

This is a usually a matter of choice. Dry food can be left out for the cat at all times, but canned food will spoil if not eaten within two hours. Store dry food in the original bag or a secure container, tightly closed, in a cool, dry, pest-proof place. Refrigerate canned food after opening.

FEEDING MOTHERS

The queen's nutrient demands start to increase early in pregnancy, rising more acutely when she is nursing kittens. She needs an abundant, high-quality diet, AAFCO-certified for reproduction and/or growth. Leave food out or feed all she will eat several times a day; monitor her weight gain.

KITTENS GROWING UP

When a kitten is three weeks old, start her on canned or dry kitten growth food mixed with cat milk replacer or water. In the next few weeks, gradually decrease the amount of liquid in the mixture. After weaning is complete at seven to nine weeks, kittens should be fed free-choice or all they will eat three or four times a day.

At about one year of age, slowly introduce kittens to an adult maintenance diet. Adults on canned food should be fed at least twice a day. Dry food may be fed free-choice, but guard against obesity.

Observe your cat's body condition. You should be able to feel, but not see, the ribs. If not, consult your veterinarian about a weight-loss program.

ENVIRONMENT

Cats are easily upset and fastidious. Feed in a peaceful, quiet place, away from household traffic patterns and litter boxes. Give each cat a separate dish. Use wide, flat, glass or ceramic dishes with low sides. Don't use plastic; cats may develop skin problems from contact with plastic dishes.

If you have to change your cat's diet, mix a small amount of the new food with the accustomed food, and slowly increase the proportion of the new over three to five days.

SUPPLEMENTS AND TREATS

Normal cats on good diets do not need supplements or treats, which may have adverse affects. For example, if milk is given in quantity, it will not only unbalance the diet but may cause diarrhea in the adult cat.

DINNER TIME

Discard leftover wet food and wash dishes after every meal. Wash and refill dry-food dishes and water bowls at least once a day.

NEVER, NEVER

The following foods should never be fed to cats:

- **Chocolate** Theobromine, a component of chocolate, is toxic to cats (and dogs). If your cat ingests chocolate, contact your veterinarian.
- **Onions** In quantity, onions can cause a blood disorder called Heinz-body anemia.
- **Raw fish, poultry or eggs** Uncooked animal products frequently carry bacteria or parasites that can cause serious illness. In addition, components of raw egg white and raw fish can destroy important vitamins.
- **Bones** Bones may splinter, causing choking or perforations of the gastrointestinal tract.
- **Dog food** Nutritionally, dog food is wrong for cats. Feed dogs and cats separately.

TRAINING TIPS

Behavioral training is the best form of training you can give your cat. Although some people do performance-train their cats, it is time-consuming and there's no guarantee of success.

TEMPTING TREATS
You can entice your cat to come by dangling a toy or offering her favorite food, but this doesn't mean she will obey every time.

OFF LIMITS
If you are unable to keep your cat from your stove, cover the top with syrup or another sticky substance. Cats, such as this Siamese, hate anything sticky on them and it won't take long for her to decide the area is off limits.

Don't try to turn your cat into a dog. If you want a pet to sit, roll over or come on command, a cat is not for you. You can train her to come for meals (all of the time) and when you call (most of the time)—success will depend entirely on her mood.

HOUSEHOLD SAFETY
The most important things to train your cat for are activities that might endanger either her or your belongings. You don't want her making the stovetop her habitat as too often she may be burned. And your guests might take a dim view of sharing your supper when it's been prepared with the help of the cat.

Begin training your cat as soon as she is old enough to try and jump up on the stove. A squirt with a spray bottle is effective, but only if you can stand guard in the kitchen

24 hours a day. For those other times, cover the surface of the stove top with metal pots and pans. Not only will it be difficult for her to find a place to squat, but the noise they make when she jumps up should send her scampering. Cats hate noise and quickly learn to avoid making any. As a matter of course, you might cover the top of your stove, refrigerator and microwave with pots to discourage her from making them her lairs.

ON THE FURNITURE
It is not practical to allow your cat access to one chair and forbid access to another. She will not understand the difference between the two chairs and you will end up with a nervous and unhappy cat. However, if you don't want her to scratch your furniture, there are several methods of training.

If you are in the room, keep a water gun or spray bottle full of water at hand and squirt her the moment she starts to scratch. If she likes the water (yes, some cats do) then throw a rolled up newspaper or a bunch of keys on the floor near her. The loud sound of the magazine or keys landing, as well as the surprise, should stop her scratching. Be sure your aim is good, and

DETERRENTS

To discourage your cat from scratching the furniture, attach orange peel to it—she will hate the smell and quickly back away.

remember, the objective is to frighten her away, not to injure her.

These methods are good only as long as you are awake and in the room. For those other times, try confining her to a room or pen so she cannot scratch the furniture. If this doesn't appeal to you, then tape orange peel to those areas where she likes to scratch. Or cover her favorite scratching areas with clear heavy plastic, available at pet stores. Another suggestion is to attach a small scratching post to either end of the couch or chair.

Don't try the trick of inflating rubber balloons and taping them to the furniture to make certain areas off limits to her. The balloons are dangerous—and even fatal—when punctured and the remnants inhaled by her.

LITTER-PAN TRAINING

A kitten will generally take to using a litter pan naturally. However, if she uses a rug or bedding as a litter pan, deter her from repeating the offense by lightly spraying the area with cologne. Most cats like to lick perfume and won't soil where they lick.

FLOWER POTS

To prevent your cat from digging up the soil in a flower pot or using it as a litter pan, cover the earth with small stones. If she persists, you should consider hanging the plant well out of her reach. Never use mothballs as a deterrent as they could be fatal to her if eaten.

CAT FLAPS

If you would like your cat to come and go at will, a cat flap may be the answer. To train her to use the cat flap, prop it completely open. Leave her in the house and position yourself outside, directly in front of the flap. Then call to her with her favorite food at hand. Once she is through, go inside and repeat the process until she willingly goes through the cat flap. Then, lower the flap halfway so she is forced to push it aside in order to pass through. Again, call her and offer a treat when she goes through. Once she is using the partially closed flap without hesitation, move on to the final step, which is to repeat the process with the flap down.

UNWANTED GUESTS

Although a cat flap is a good way to allow your own cat access, it is also an invitation to neighboring cats. To avoid this, you can buy an electronic or magnetized cat flap that can be activated only by a special collar worn by your cat.

WHILE YOU'RE AWAY

Cats don't like change and don't travel well, so whenever possible make arrangements for your cat to stay at home in her own surroundings and avoid sending her anywhere to board.

water feeder

dry-food feeder

Cats don't travel well and much prefer the familiar comforts of their home and surroundings. They will generally be much happier and safer if left at home, but you will also need to consider how long you will be gone, where you live and the state of your finances.

HOME ALONE

If your cats live totally outdoors, then oversize self-feeders for both dry food and water will suffice if you are away for short periods. The amount of both will depend on the number of cats you have and the length of time you expect to be away.

Or, to make sure they have a fresh water supply, you might try one of those self-waterers that attach directly to the water faucet.

If you have several indoor cats, and they are all in good health and do not require extra meals or medication, you can safely leave them alone for a few days. Be advised though that they may rearrange your house while you are away, so it is best to confine them to one area. Again, self-feeders for food and water are ideal. Make sure the water cannot spill (tip-proof water bowls are available as well as water-feeder containers), and be sure to leave extra litter pans.

PET-SITTERS

If you have kittens or older or sick cats needing extra meals and attention, it is best to have someone come in to care for them. Many neighborhoods have an exchange for pet-sitting. If an exchange is not possible, it's better to hire someone to pet-sit for you than ask a friend or relative to do so. While they may be glad to help out in an emergency, if you make this a routine request and they do not take care of the cats properly, you have no recourse short of losing their friendship should you complain.

In the more populated areas, you can easily find professional pet-sitters. They will come to your house once or twice a day, feed and water the cats, play with them and

INDOOR CATTERY
If you cannot leave your cat at home, a boarding kennel is another option.

change their litter pan. Most pet-sitters will also bring in your mail and newspaper and water your indoor plants. Some even offer report cards on your cat.

BOARDING

Your other alternative to a pet-sitter is to leave your cat with a friend or to board her with a veterinarian or boarding kennel. However, cats dislike change and may not do well away from home. And if you leave her with a friend who has cats, she may not mix well with the cats and so will have to be kept alone in a room. Always check out facilities before leaving your cat.

ROAD TRAVEL

If you do have to transport your cat, perhaps because you are moving, always confine her in a suitable carrying cage. If it makes you feel better, when you stop for a rest break, offer her food, water and access to a litter pan. Don't be surprised if she refuses all three. Most cats prefer to wait until they reach the motel—or the new home—before eating, drinking or going to the bathroom. Don't worry—she can survive very well during the day.

RAIL AND AIR TRAVEL

If you are shipping cats by rail or air, first check with the carriers and find out their rules for health certificates and suitable shipping containers. It is not advisable to give cats tranquilizers. Some cats can become very aggressive

on this type of medication while others become sick. If heavily tranquilized, their vomiting can cause them to drown in their own fluids.

Line the bottom of the shipping container with a good thickness of newspaper and tear up strips of newspaper, filling the container about halfway to the top. This makes an excellent insulator for heat and cold and your cat can burrow into it for security. Should she have to go to the bathroom, she can cover her waste with the strips of paper.

Always make a definite reservation for her with the airline or train carrier and have a back-up plan in mind. Always try for a direct flight with no change of plane or train. Most airlines will not carry pets if the ground temperature at either departure or destination is below 45°F (7°C) or above 80°F (27°C), but you will need to check on this with the airline when you book.

open-top carrier

airline carrier

OUTDOOR CATTERY

Some boarding kennels have areas that allow cats outdoor access. Always check out a new kennel with a visit before your cat's stay.

51

HEALTH CARE

*Cats are rather delicate creatures and they
are subject to a good many different
ailments, but I never heard of one who
suffered from insomnia.*

JOSEPH WOOD KRUTCH (1893-1970),
American author, teacher, critic and naturalist

THE HEALTHY CAT

✚

When stroking or grooming your cat, take the opportunity to look for
any physical health problems. The earlier you detect anything, the
easier it should be for the veterinarian to treat your cat successfully.

• Look inside your cat's ears to see if there is a dark brown crusty substance or any other sign of ear mites.

• Gently pull on the skin across his shoulders or back. If it stands out, or is slow to fall back into place, he may be suffering from dehydration, especially if other signs of disease are present.

• Your cat's eyes should be clear and clean. The appearance of the third eyelid, or haw, may indicate that your cat is sick.

• Carefully check inside your cat's mouth. His breath should be fresh and there should be no sign of gum disease.

• Have you noticed your cat scratching himself more than usual, particularly around the head and rear? If so, he may be suffering from fleas or other external parasites.

• To see if your cat is the proper weight, run your hands down his backbone and across his hip bones and lower abdomen. You should be able to feel his ribs easily, but not see them.

• Look for cuts on your cat's paws or any damage to his nails. Do his claws need trimming?

• Gently feel your cat's body. Lumps may indicate an abscess, particularly if he ventures outdoors, or a tumor. Most tumors detected will be benign, but you should have the veterinarian check him.

Your cat keeps to a fairly regular routine, and so you may be able to notice signs that could alert you to possible health problems. Signs to watch out for include:
• Change in everyday routine
• Listlessness
• Behavioral changes
• Excessive scratching
• Excessive cleaning
• Appearance of the third eyelid
• Weight loss
• Decreased appetite
• Decreased thirst
• Increased appetite
• Increased thirst
• Diarrhea
• Constipation
• Blood in feces
• Increased urination
• Straining while urinating
• Bloody urine
• Vomiting
• Bad breath
• Distended stomach
• Watery eyes
• Sneezing or coughing
• Difficulty breathing
• Dull coat
• Pale gums

• Examine your cat's rear end. It should be clean and healthy. If there are signs of inflammation, he may be suffering from diarrhea and if it persists, he should be taken to the veterinarian.

• Take a look at your male cat's tail. If there is a build-up of a brown secretion and some swelling or hair loss around the base of his tail, he is suffering from stud tail.

• Is your cat not as agile as he used to be, and is he showing signs of stiffness in his joints? This may be nothing more than old age, but you should check with your veterinarian.

HEALTH CARE BASICS

You may be able to tell if your cat is sick by watching his body language and noticing any variation in his everyday routine. Observant owners can often detect signs of illness at a very early stage and take the cat to the veterinarian before the situation becomes too serious.

There are many signs that indicate your cat is unwell. If he is listless and does not greet you normally, if he stops eating his favorite food or if his normally sleek and shiny coat is dull and open, he is probably in distress. Other symptoms may include a change in his normal behavior or a change in the third eyelid, or haw.

Some changes in behavior are more subtle and harder to spot unless we pay careful attention. Does your normally outgoing female cat start hissing when you pet her? This could be a sign of a uterine infection (see p. 64) or a bladder problem. Does your shy and retiring older cat suddenly start attacking other cats even when not provoked? This, too, is a sign that something is wrong. The causes may range from nothing more than an infected tooth to a tumor.

And what about your three-month-old kitten? Has he stopped chasing his tail or pouncing on your toes? Has his appetite declined? If so, you should see these as alarm signals alerting you to take him to the veterinarian. In a three-month-old it may be nothing more than normal teething, but it is best to have your veterinarian check him.

HOME CARE

When your cat is ill, the most important thing you can do is keep him warm, quiet, well-fed and watered. Cats dislike noise and bright lights and seek secluded areas when they are sick. For the indoor cat, set up a retreat in a room not used by members of your family or other pets. A soft towel lining a cardboard box and placed on the floor of a closet is ideal. With the door slightly ajar, the cat has darkness and solitude. For the outdoor cat, line a tire with an old blanket in the garage, making sure there are no drafts. To keep your cat warm, heating pads and hot water bottles (not too hot!) may be effective, or you can cut the foot off a sock and make a "sweater" to keep him warm.

DAILY ROUTINES

When a cat is feeling well, he eats his food, uses his litter pan and follows a fairly routine schedule of playing and sleeping. Any major change in this routine could signal a health problem.

THIRD EYELID

The third eyelid, or haw, consists of a membrane in the corner of the eye nearest the nose. It is not usually visible in a healthy cat, but may appear when your cat is sick, partially covering the eye. It is either white or pink in color.

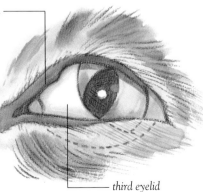

upper eyelid

third eyelid

In addition to administering any medication prescribed by your veterinarian, you need to supply your cat with plenty of fluids. If your cat is not drinking and does not seem his normal self, contact your veterinarian. You may be advised to force fluids into his mouth with an eye dropper or plastic syringe, but be careful because the fluid can be forced into the lungs and result in pneumonia.

If he clamps his teeth down firmly on the dropper and won't open his mouth, insert the tip through the side of his mouth. You will find an opening there and can squirt in the water.

Clear chicken broth and the juices from cooked meat can also be used as fluids. These have the advantage of making your cat thirsty, prompting him to drink on his own.

If he is dehydrated, your veterinarian may need to administer fluids under the cat's skin or into a vein. There will be other signs of illness in such a case.

You should also ensure your cat eats enough, particularly if he has a respiratory infection. When cats have respiratory infections, they cannot smell, and when cats cannot smell, they do not eat. Place a small dab of food on your finger and insert it in his mouth. Sometimes this is all it takes for his instinct to take over.

If he still won't eat, contact your veterinarian. He or she may be able to prescribe a complete diet than can be syringe-fed to your sick cat.

Cats hate to be dirty. When they are sick, they don't want to clean themselves, so it is up to you to do it for them. Start with a soft cloth dampened with warm water. Gently clean his eyes and nose and around his mouth. And don't forget his rear end because he may be too sick to clean himself after using the litter pan. Refrain from using soap or other cleaning agents. In severe cases, try brushing him gently or using a dry shampoo. Usually, though, when your cat is sick, just the sound of your soothing voice and the touch of your gentle hands will do wonders for his recovery.

DRINKING ASSISTANCE

To prevent your cat from becoming dehydrated, your veterinarian may advise you to give him fluids. Gently insert a dropper filled with liquid into his mouth, and repeat regularly until he is drinking by himself.

CLEAN LICKING

If your cat is not eating, try putting some food on one of his paws. Cats hate to be dirty, and he will probably lick it off right away.

57

VACCINATION

✚

Many serious, even potentially fatal, illnesses can be prevented by vaccination. Some inoculations are compulsory while some are optional, but it is essential that you check with your veterinarian for the best course of preventive medicine.

A HEALTHY PET

It is compulsory for all cats to be immunized against a number of diseases. If you are acquiring a cat, be sure to check that, as with this Ocicat, all his vaccinations are in order.

It is essential that you visit the veterinarian and get a complete check-up for your new cat, including the vaccinations and preventive medical procedures described in this section.

All cats are susceptible to, and must be immunized against, several serious viral and bacterial diseases. These are feline infectious enteritis (FIE), also known as panleukopenia, an often fatal infection of the intestines, causing loss of appetite, fever, vomiting and diarrhea; feline calicivirus (FCV), an infection that causes respiratory tract disease similar to a human cold; and feline rhinotracheitis (FVR), also known as "cat flu." It is highly recommended that the initial vaccinations for these be given at 8 and 12 weeks of age, preferably using the modified live vaccine, available in either injection-form or nose drops.

Exceptions to the above schedule are when you have an orphan kitten who is not building up immunities from his mother's milk, or if you have a large colony of cats and want them to be protected earlier.

After your kitten has been vaccinated twice against FIE, FCV, FVR and chlamydia, a highly contagious bacterial disease, he will not require another booster of these vaccines until he is a year old.

VACCINATION SCHEDULE

Although there are some vaccinations that are compulsory for all cats, it is important that you talk to your veterinarian about any others your cat may require, depending on his breed, whether he is an indoor or an outdoor cat and the environment to which he is exposed.

DISEASE	AGE AT FIRST SHOT	AGE AT SECOND SHOT	BOOSTER
Panleukopenia	8–10 weeks	12–16 weeks	12 months
Viral rhinotracheitis	8–10 weeks	12–16 weeks	12 months
Caliciviral disease	8–10 weeks	12–16 weeks	12 months
Pneumonitis (Chlamydiosis)	8–10 weeks	12–16 weeks	12 months
Rabies	12 weeks	64 weeks	12 or 36 months
Feline Leukemia	10 weeks*	12 & 24 weeks*	13-14 months*
Feline Infectious Peritonitis	16 weeks*	20 weeks*	12 months*

* Optional

Source: American Veterinary Medical Association

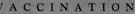

FeLV, FIP and Rabies

Cats can also be vaccinated against feline leukemia virus (FeLV), a complex and often fatal virus that can attack the bone marrow and can cause cancer; and feline infectious peritonitis (FIP), a disease that causes the chest or abdominal cavity to fill up with fluid. These vaccinations may not be necessary for isolated indoor cats, which are unlikely to be exposed to these diseases.

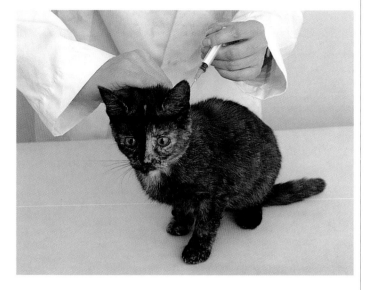

Although the chance of exposure of indoor cats to rabies is very small, all cats should be vaccinated against the disease. Rabies is essentially always fatal to cats and humans. By vaccinating their pets, responsible pet owners are protecting their animals, their neighbors and themselves.

Expert Advice

It is also best to consult with your veterinarian as to the best course of vaccinations for your particular cat or cats and the unique conditions in your household. For example, if you have a cat with a short nose and flat face, such as a Persian or an Exotic, who, due to reduced nasal capacity can be more prone to respiratory problems, your veterinarian may choose to vaccinate earlier or more frequently. And the breeding queen, the male stud and the cat exhibited at shows may require more frequent boosters because they have a higher exposure to many diseases. On the other hand, the single cat living totally indoors may not require the same vaccinations as an outdoor cat or a cat from a multiple-cat household.

Medical Records

If you did not receive a complete health and vaccination record when you acquired your adult cat, your veterinarian will help prepare a record for you, which will be the cat's medical history throughout his life. On your kitten's first visit, your veterinarian will start his medical record.

ANNUAL CHECKUPS

Always ensure that you take your cat to the veterinarian for his annual checkup. Not only will he be given any vaccinations or booster shots necessary, but your veterinarian will also check that the cat is not suffering from any other diseases or ailments.

SYRINGE AND VACCINE VIAL

Vaccinations are carried out by your veterinarian. Although they are normally given by injection, some may also be given in the form of nose drops.

INTERNAL PARASITES

✚

Most internal parasites live in the intestines of their host. While they can be common among cats and most are no cause for serious concern, you should contact the veterinarian if you suspect that your cat is suffering from them.

roundworms

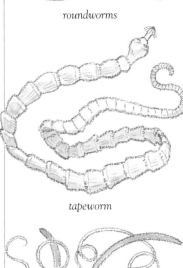

tapeworm

whipworms

All these common parasites can be found by having your veterinarian examine a fecal sample. For information on heartworm, see p. 69.

ROUNDWORMS

These are a common feline parasite that are either passed on from the mother or picked up by contact with infected soil or by eating infected rodents. They can quickly multiply into large colonies and look like long strings of spaghetti. Adult roundworms live in the small intestine. Eggs can survive in soil for years. After hatching, the larvae sometimes move on to the lungs. Although symptoms of infestation are not always visible, they may include vomiting, diarrhea and a distended stomach.

All cats are susceptible to roundworms, but the greatest danger is to kittens. Even if the mother is not passing eggs in her feces, infective larvae may still be hidden in her body tissues. When she produces milk for her kittens, she infects them via the mammary glands. Very often a check by the veterinarian will not find evidence of roundworms in the kittens because they have not yet reached the intestines. Have a second examination 10 to 14 days after the first to make sure there are still none. If the queen is treated with one of the effective drugs prior to breeding, it may decrease the infection rate for kittens.

TAPEWORM

Another common parasite in cats is the tapeworm, which feeds on nutrients in the digestive tract. All that is visible to the naked eye is the segment, resembling a piece of rice, as it is broken off and expelled through the anus. More often than not, there are no other visible symptoms.

The indoor cat can be infected through fleas, and the outdoor cat not only through fleas but by eating rodents or rabbits. The best preventive is controlling fleas

MOTHER AND KITTENS
A female queen infected with roundworms will pass them on to her litter while nursing.

and limiting hunting in outdoor cats. If you see evidence of tapeworm, such as segments in his feces, he should be examined and treated by the veterinarian. Indoor cats are not as likely to be exposed to the parasites.

HOOKWORMS

Infestations with hookworms are less common in cats than in dogs. Weakness, anemia and diarrhea are some of the signs of hookworms. Hookworms should be treated and your veterinarian will prescribe medicine, but the only preventive measure is to keep your cat indoors.

TOXOPLASMA

Many cats at some time acquire the intestinal parasite toxoplasma, a type of protozoa. It can be passed from mothers to kittens, or picked up through hunting, or by contact with feces from infected cats. Most cats exhibit no symptoms, develop natural immunity, and are not threatened by the disease. Some, however, can become ill or even die, especially if infected before birth or if they have concurrent illnesses. Many humans are exposed to toxoplasmosis, with the only symptom being a mild stomach upset. They, too, have developed immunity.

The main danger of toxoplasmosis is to pregnant women as it can cause miscarriage and birth defects, but there is little danger if simple sanitary precautions are taken. For a pregnant woman to become infected, she would have to handle cat feces and then touch her mouth or nose with dirty hands. Or she could catch the disease by handling raw meat without washing afterward, or by eating meat not thoroughly cooked. To avoid any possibility of danger, use protective gloves when changing your cat's litter pan.

COCCIDIA

An indoor cat may have contracted this disease as a kitten in his previous home, or by eating infected mice, birds or rabbits, or through contact with feces from infected cats. Overcrowding in cat colonies or breeders' catteries coupled with poor sanitation contribute to the spread of this pest.

If your cat is off his feed and has diarrhea, have him checked for coccidiosis. Other signs may be listlessness, lack of energy and weight loss.

Strict hygiene and medication as prescribed by the veterinarian can alleviate signs of the disease in the indoor cat. The same treatment will apply to the outdoor cat, but eradication is almost impossible as he may continue to be reinfected. A combination of coccidiosis and roundworms can be fatal in kittens, so seek prompt medical attention if your kitten shows symptoms.

OUTDOOR LIFE
There is little you can do to prevent a recurrence of internal parasites if your cat ventures outdoors, but prompt treatment will minimize the damage.

DOCTOR IN THE HOME
Your veterinarian might prescribe a course of pills or some worming paste to treat your cat. If you have trouble administering them, a pill-popper may be of help for the pills and a syringe for the paste.

EXTERNAL PARASITES

✚

External parasites live on the skin of your cat and feed on both his skin and blood, causing discomfort and, in some cases, sickness. They are a common problem for cats, particularly those that go outdoors, but your cat is easily treated and will recover quickly.

FLEA COLLARS
If your kitten goes outdoors, he may pick up fleas. You may want to purchase a flea collar to help prevent an infestation, but other treatments can be more effective.

TO THE VETERINARIAN
If your cat scratches his ears excessively, he may have ear mites. Your veterinarian can examine him and prescribe the appropriate treatment.

FLEAS
Many cats are highly sensitive to fleas. Some cats will react to the presence of a single flea not only by scratching vigorously but also by losing great patches of hair. Fleas tend to be more prevalent around the eyes, ears and anus, and a cat will scratch, suffer hair loss and be thoroughly miserable.

When combating fleas—and it is combat—you will need to treat your cat repeatedly as well as ridding his quarters and/or your living quarters of fleas. You must fumigate the area again within 10 to 14 days after the first treatment as that is when the eggs hatch and a new crop of fleas emerges.

Some of the newer flea remedies include monthly pills or skin drops that are available only through your veterinarian. Other remedies include flea collars, powders, sprays and baths. Always ask your veterinarian about the advisability of combining flea remedies, or you might poison your cat.

If you have indoor cats and a dog that goes outdoors into an enclosed yard, you can either hire a professional flea exterminator to spray your yard monthly, or you can purchase the equipment and do it yourself. If there are no fleas in the yard, the dog can't bring them into the house.

While it is not difficult to rid your indoor pet and your house of fleas, it may be impossible to rid an outdoor cat of them.

Fleas not only carry tapeworms but may give your cat feline infectious anemia (FIA), a disease that can result in anemia and a very sick cat. Symptoms include pale gums and a high temperature, but your veterinarian will take a blood test to make a definite diagnosis, and will then prescribe the necessary treatment for your cat.

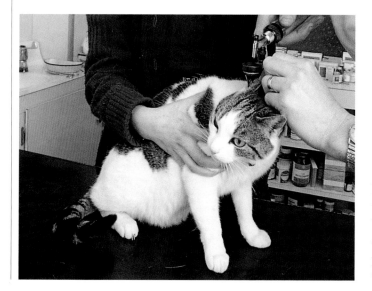

EAR MITES

If you notice a dark brown waxy substance in your cat's ears, or if he torments himself by repeatedly scratching his ears, he may have ear mites. These are microscopic parasites that live in the ear canal and feed on skin and debris therein.

To make absolutely sure that ear mites are the problem, take your cat to the veterinarian for examination and treatment. Your veterinarian can recommend the application of medication to eradicate them. You may need to repeat the treatment several times as mites are persistent.

Alternatively, if you have a multiple-cat household or are caring for stray or feral cats and cannot reasonably take them all to the veterinarian, you may be able to treat the mites at home. Simply dip a cotton swab into boric-acid powder, and gently clean the visible part of the inside of the ear only. The advantage of the dry powder is that it suffocates the mites and kills them without leaving a messy oil in your cat's ears that could make him even more miserable. It should also protect against other mites entering his ears.

TICKS, MITES AND MANGE

Ticks and mites are not often found on the indoor cat. If your indoor cat does have signs of any of these parasites, they have probably been carried in on dogs or human clothing. Outdoor and sick cats are most susceptible because they are more likely to be in contact with infected cats. If you detect a tick on your cat, do not attempt to burn it off or pluck it out. A simple remedy is to cover it with petroleum jelly and leave it. The tick will usually die and fall off within a day or two.

Mites are parasites that are not usually seen with the naked eye. Mite infestation causes mange, which may include itchiness, dandruff and bald patches all over the cat's body. These signs may also be indicative of an allergic reaction or a hormonal change. If your cat has these signs, you should take him to the veterinarian who can prescribe treatment. Treatment for mange usually involves medicated dips or baths at home.

Although not a common problem among cats, cats from multiple-cat environments often continue to be reinfected.

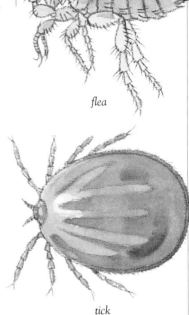

flea

tick

mange mite

CAT SCRATCHING
Don't jump to conclusions just because your cat is scratching himself. All cats scratch and it does not necessarily mean he's infested with external parasites.

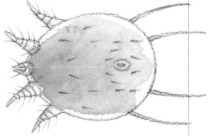

COMMON HEALTH PROBLEMS

✚

It is inevitable that your cat will, over the course of his life, become sick. Although most ailments are easily treated, some can be fatal, so it is important to be alert to any signs of disease.

HAZARD FOR QUEEN
If, like this Korat, your female cat is unaltered, she will be susceptible to pyometra, an infection of the uterus.

CAREFUL WATCH
You should keep a close eye out for any changes in your cat's behavior. If you notice he is having trouble urinating and is licking his genital area more than usual, take him to the veterinarian at once. It could be a sign that your cat is suffering from feline lower urinary tract disorder (FLUTD).

PYOMETRA

Pyometra is an infection of the uterus that attacks unaltered female cats. Signs may include listlessness, lack of appetite, great thirst and frequent urination, as well as an odorous discharge from the vagina that is thick and creamy. However, some females exhibit no signs at all—her coat may be shiny, her eyes clear and her appetite and behavior normal. And, since cats are so clean, you have to keep a close watch for any signs of vaginal discharge before she cleans it away.

However, there are signs to alert you to the increased possibility of pyometra. If your cat has frequent seasons, or if her seasons are few and far between, she will be more susceptible to pyometra. Or if she has mated, you may think she is pregnant when it is really the infection in the uterus causing her abdomen to appear plump with kittens.

The instant you spot the discharge take her to the veterinarian. She can die if not treated immediately, as the infection can cause the uterus to burst. The most effective treatment for pyometra is ovariohysterectomy, the removal of both uterus and ovaries.

FELINE LOWER URINARY TRACT DISORDER (FLUTD)

If your cat is having trouble urinating, if you see him straining in a squatting position or if there is blood in his urine, take him to the veterinarian at once. He could have FLUTD.

Other signs include not using the litter pan, incontinence and frequent licking of the genital area. If your cat's urinary tract is blocked, he will die without immediate treatment.

It is not known what causes FLUTD, or why episodes recur. Urinary stones are one cause and cystitis, a urethral plug or a tumor may be others. Although we don't know yet how to prevent it, increasing the water intake, and decreasing stress, may help. Most importantly, feeding a cat food that results in acidic urine and is low in magnesium can help to maintain urinary tract health.

ADMINISTERING A PILL

Now we face the difficult chore of giving your cat a pill. By following the steps outlined, it will be easier for both of you.

If your cat struggles, have someone else hold him while you insert the pill. Or place him on either a window or door screen and lightly press your body against his to help restrain him. He will cling to the screen with his nails and you will have both hands free to administer the pill. As a last resort try wrapping him in a blanket but be very careful as he may struggle even more.

Some cats will never let you open their mouth, so if the pill is not coated, mash it with a spoon. It can then be mixed either with water, broth or food.

OPEN WIDE
Open your cat's mouth by placing one hand on his upper jaw and pushing down his lower jaw with your other hand.

INSERTING THE PILL
Insert the pill well back in the mouth either using the fingers of your lower hand or with the aid of a pill-popper. Blowing on his nose may make him swallow.

PINCHING THE THROAT
Close his mouth and, to encourage him to swallow the pill, try stroking his throat. If he doesn't swallow the pill, pinch the skin on his throat and pull it outward. This will stimulate him to swallow.

ADMINISTERING EAR DROPS
If your cat suffers from ear mites, put the drops into his ear as instructed by your veterinarian, then gently massage his ear for a few seconds.

RESPIRATORY AILMENTS

Cats are prone to respiratory problems. Although you have already protected your cat against the serious "cat flu," or FVR (see p. 58), he is still susceptible to other infections.

Early signs of respiratory ailments include watery eyes, sneezing and coughing. You should take your cat to the veterinarian as soon as these signs appear or nose and chest congestion develop. Your veterinarian may prescribe a course of antibiotics (be sure to finish the entire course; no stopping just because the signs seem to have gone away). The cat may also need eye drops or nose drops. If he is severely congested, you may be advised to try a bulb-type aspirator.

Although the veterinarian will give the medication that is best for your cat's illness, it is up to you to provide the tender loving care. You may need to coax the cat to eat and he will usually recover far more quickly at home than in the hospital. Be sure to follow the general care recommendations (see pp. 56–57).

ALLERGIES AND ADVERSE REACTIONS

A cat's immune system reacts negatively when he is exposed to substances his body considers foreign. The substance which does the provoking is called an antigen. It can be any substance capable of producing a detectable immune response. An allergen is an antigen that produces an allergic response. Anything that might cause you to sniffle, cough, wheeze or itch can have the same effect on your cat. In addition to external stimulants, cats can have allergic reactions to vaccinations, food ingredients and medications.

ADMINISTERING NOSE DROPS
Hold your cat gently but firmly while you administer nose drops. Then continue to hold his head in a tilted position until you are sure the drops have been successfully administered.

ADMINISTERING EYE DROPS

After applying ointment or liquid to your cat's eyes, hold him loosely for a few moments to let the liquid do its job; otherwise, he will immediately rub it out.

Cats are most commonly allergic to flea bites. Signs of allergic reactions can include itching and hair loss. Flea bite allergies affect cats of both sexes and all breeds, and is most common among cats between the ages of 3 and 5 years old. If your cat shows any signs of flea allergies, your veterinarian can prescribe a special diet and/or drug treatment.

Cats may also react to common chemicals. Cleaning agents, such as bleach and ammonia, should never be used near your cat unless diluted, and then only where there is proper ventilation and the area can be thoroughly dried afterward.

Cats can be sensitive to flea preventives or control remedies. And, if you use powder to help groom your longhaired cat, he may sneeze and his eyes may water just as yours might. At cat shows, by the end of the day, a walk down an aisle filled with longhaired cats is accompanied by the sounds of snorting and coughing and the sight of watering eyes, all because of the hair flying through the air and the various powders and sprays applied to the coats.

Hand in hand with allergies is the possibility that your cat may develop a type of asthma. With your veterinarian's help to control this, your pet can still live a comfortable life.

WELL GERMS

When you introduce a new kitten or cat to your home, and you already have one or more cats, you should be aware that the new addition may not be immune to the "well germs" carried by your present cats. Even though your other cats have received all of their shots and are in good health, they have become accustomed to the germs in their environment and have built up immunity to them. Having come from another environment, your new cat may not be immune to these germs and may come down with a respiratory infection or some other ailment within a week or two. Your other cats, in turn, may not be immune to the "well germs" of your new cat, so you may see minor illnesses in all your cats as they adjust.

TRANSMITTING RINGWORM
Ringworm is one of the few diseases that can be passed from cats to humans, with children being most susceptible.

RINGWORM

Scratching, biting, and excessive washing of his coat can signal a number of different skin problems for your cat, including the stubborn condition of ringworm. Oddly enough, ringworm is not caused by a worm at all, but by a parasitic fungus. It can be transmitted through contact with infected animals, soil or even humans. Kittens, pregnant queens and frail and elderly cats are most susceptible to the disease.

Signs of ringworm on your cat can include a few broken hairs around the muzzle or ears as well as small, usually round, bald patches that later become crusty. Although most patches are found on the head, ears, paws and tail, they can appear anywhere on your cat's body. If you have an indoor/outdoor cat, or a multiple-cat household, you might mistake the first signs of ringworm for a scratch or bite inflicted by another cat.

If you suspect your cat has ringworm, you should take him to the veterinarian. The disease is usually treated with pills and/or topical treatments. For an indoor cat, you should also vacuum the cat's living quarters and wash his bedding, toys and other things that might harbor the fungus. Treating the environment obviously is impossible with the indoor/outdoor cat or in totally outdoor cat colonies.

Although some cats are carriers of ringworm, many develop natural immunity to the disease. Since the carriers do not show any signs, it may be very difficult to track down and treat the cause of the recurring ringworm in a multiple-cat household.

Cats can transmit ringworm to humans and dogs, and humans and dogs can transmit the disease to cats. If your cat is infected with ringworm, extreme care should be taken with handling him. If possible, isolate him until the scabs fall off the affected areas, taking with them the hairs that contain the spores.

BE ALERT
If your cat is scratching more than usual, take a close look at his coat, and see if there are any round, bald patches or other signs that may indicate he is suffering from ringworm. If so, he will need to be treated by the veterinarian.

HEARTWORM

Feline Heartworm Disease (FHD) is rare, but can be life-threatening. It is caused by parasites entering the bloodstream through the bite of an infected mosquito, and the parasites then migrate to the heart and pulmonary arteries where they mature.

All cats are at risk, but those with exposure to mosquitoes are at highest risk. Warm, humid climates are ideal conditions for heartworms. And your cat doesn't have to go outside to be bitten by mosquitoes. In fact, studies indicate that indoor cats may be more likely to pick up an FHD infection.

Unfortunately, the symptoms of FHD in cats are vague and can differ markedly from the canine version. Researchers believe cats with heartworms may be misdiagnosed with feline asthma, or may develop asthma as a consequence of FHD. Aside from asthma, other signs include weight loss, weakness and collapse.

At present there is no definitive test for FHD in cats, although blood tests may be helpful. A preventive treatment for heartworm disease is available from veterinarians.

ACNE

Surprisingly, cats can suffer from acne. It is generally found under the chin and around the mouth. This was originally called "Aby chin" because it was first diagnosed in the Abyssinian breed as it readily showed up on their white chins. Later it was learned that any cat can get acne.

It's a good idea to examine the chin area of your dark-colored cats to see if you can see or feel slight crusty bumps. These are easily seen on white or light-colored cats and look like coffee grains. Wash the affected area with a mild soap, rinse thoroughly with warm water and dry, dry, dry. Since acne thrives in damp places, you can help the drying process by rubbing cornstarch on light-colored cats or fuller's earth on dark ones.

Causes of acne may range from eating from plastic dishes to food becoming embedded in the chin. Since cats continue to eat, the possibility of them having acne is ongoing, but a careful check of the chin and weekly washings can keep your cat pimple-free. If there are any signs of infection, such as redness, swelling, or discharge, contact your veterinarian.

BETTER SAFE THAN SORRY

Little is known about heartworm in cats and the signs are vague. So, if your cat, like the Burmese below, is feeling sick, take him to the veterinarian immediately.

PROBLEM SKIN

To prevent acne, try serving your cat's meals in a nonplastic food dish. Then make sure you wash his chin regularly to clear away any food remnants.

ELIZABETHAN COLLAR

If your cat is recovering from surgery and you don't want him to pull out his stitches, or if he has a wound that must be kept bandaged, you will need to fit him with an Elizabethan collar (so called because it looks like the round collars worn by women in the Elizabethan age). Otherwise, you will find that he can contort himself like a pretzel to reach every location on his body and will work steadily to remove the offending stitches or bandages.

Your veterinarian will provide you with such a collar or you can make one at home. Simply take a sturdy but flexible material, such as cardboard, and cut out a circle. Cut out a smaller circle in the center, slightly larger than the size of his neck to provide room for movement. Be careful not to give him too much room or he will slip his head through and remove the collar. Then cut away about a quarter of the circle all the way through to the center opening. Punch a double row of matching holes on either side of the gap. Make cuts around the inner circle about ½ inch (2.5 cm) apart. These allow the edge to bend for a snug fit. Place the collar around his neck and use a piece of string to lace the open sides together.

pattern for an Elizabethan collar

lacing the collar up

ABSCESSES

Abscesses are hidden dangers. We often cannot see them, but we can feel them. If your cat shows no external sign of a wound, but is listless, off his eating schedule, has a dry, open coat or is not acting normally, there is a chance he is suffering from an abscess.

This is a tricky and potentially deadly situation because the skin will close over an open wound, leaving no visible sign. If your fingers do detect a lump anywhere on your cat, it could be an abscess. It is best to take the cat to the veterinarian, who can drain the abscess surgically and prescribe antibiotics. Most abscesses are the result of cat fights, and are most common in unneutered, outdoor male cats. To decrease the likelihood of your cat developing an abscess, spaying or neutering, limiting access to outdoors, and supervising interactions with other cats can be helpful.

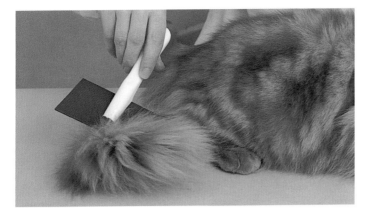

EASING THE PAIN OF STUD TAIL
Besides washing and drying
the affected area regularly
and then combing your cat's
tail thoroughly, there is little
you can do to treat stud tail.

STUD TAIL

Stud tail is so called because it is generally found in the unaltered tomcat, although it can affect females. It is the build-up of a brown secretion caused by the release of oils from the gland on the upper surface of the cat's tail, near the base. You may also notice swelling, blistering and hair loss in this area.

This condition can be controlled easily by washing and completely drying the affected area on a regular basis. If the skin is red and sore, your veterinarian may prescribe a balm to apply.

As long as your cat remains unaltered, he will continue to secrete excessive oil from the glands at the base of the tail so vigilance is necessary to keep him comfortable.

DANDRUFF

Just like you, your cat may develop dandruff, and for just about as many reasons. If he is light-colored, you may not notice the dandruff, but if his coat is dark, you will be able to see the dandruff clearly. In either case, simply petting or brushing him will bring the dandruff to the surface.

Don't panic if you see a small amount of dandruff. This is normal because the skin changes and is shed periodically. However, if the condition is severe, have him checked by the veterinarian. Excessive dandruff can be associated with almost any skin condition.

Altered cats and older cats tend to have more dandruff than unaltered and younger ones. The natural process of aging will probably cause your cat to gradually develop a thicker and drier coat and scaly skin, which might cause dandruff. Feeding a complete and balanced diet with omega-6 and omega-3 fatty acids may be helpful. You will probably not be able to cure the dandruff completely but you may be able to control it.

FLAKING SKIN
You will easily be able to detect dandruff on your dark-colored cat. However, if your cat has a light-colored coat, you may have to inspect it more closely. Either way, regular combing of his coat should help this skin condition.

71

A BALL OF FUN
Although it's difficult to stop your cat from chewing wool, you could make his habit less destructive by giving him his own ball of wool.

NEWCOMERS
If you have a multi-cat household, and one of those cats has a new litter of kittens, you might find that some of the other cats are unhappy with the additional company and start spraying.

WOOL-CHEWING

Some cats are wool-chewers. This is a loose description that encompasses cats who not only chew wool but chew towels, socks and blankets as well. Most chewers are either Siamese or part-Siamese and they start chewing as soon as they have teeth. The easiest solution is to remove temptation by either putting these possessions away or by not letting your cat into areas where they are kept. It is just about impossible to stop a wool-chewer from chewing.

And sometimes he will chew on himself! Some cats, and not just Siamese, suck on their tails much like a baby sucks on his thumb. He may also nurse on himself or other adult cats. You can break him of this habit by applying a bitter tasting liquid to his tail and other areas where he chews. If you let him chew on his tail unchecked, he could cause such mutilation that part of the tail is chewed off.

SPRAYING

Spraying is an instinctive natural act whereby cats squirt urine on vertical surfaces, generally to mark territory. It is most common in the unaltered male who will spray to attract females and warn off other tomcats. Unaltered females spray to a lesser extent, usually to attract tomcats. There is really nothing that you can do to stop an unaltered cat from spraying.

A neutered male or a spayed female may not spray for the same reasons as an unaltered cat, but could spray on occasion. If you move, change your routine or go on vacation, your altered pet may show his frustration by spraying on your furniture. Other things that might induce him to spray are the mating seasons—spring and fall—when he can hear and smell the unaltered males and females mating.

Another common reason altered cats spray is because you have acquired one cat too many, or one of your cats has a new litter of kittens. They spray because they are stressed. This is an instinctive reflex on their part and you should not punish them. They will stop spraying when the kittens go to their new homes, or when, in time, they have accepted the addition of the new cat. If spraying continues to be a problem, contact your veterinarian for advice.

SHEDDING

While outdoor cats may shed only twice a year, indoor cats may shed hair for the entire year. This is due to the fairly consistent temperature found inside the house. Older cats tend to shed more than younger

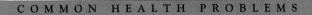

ones because they usually have a drier coat. If you suspect that your cat's shedding is excessive, you should take him to the veterinarian. If no illness is diagnosed, the shedding may be caused by a hormonal imbalance. Most likely, though, it may be caused by illness, skin allergy or parasites. Daily combing and brushing, combined with hand-grooming and an occasional bath, may help control the problem.

HAIRBALLS

If your cat has lost his appetite, has constipation and bowel problems or is vomiting, he could be suffering from hairballs. These are formed by your cat swallowing hair while cleaning and grooming himself. The hair forms into cylindrical shapes in the stomach, and is then vomited up. Many cats will choose your best chair, your bed, or the living-room rug to relieve themselves of a hairball. Hairballs are more common in longhaired cats and when cats are shedding excessively.

Daily combing combined with the occasional bath can aid in controlling hairballs. There are also hairball remedies on the market that you can administer to your cat on a weekly basis. These help the cat eliminate any hairballs by lubricating the intestines, thereby allowing the easy passage of the hairball. Feeding a diet that contains a moderately fermentable fiber

source, such as beet pulp, also may be helpful in keeping your cat's intestinal tract healthy.

Although a cat that is vomiting may simply have a hairball or have eaten grass, this can be a sign of a more serious illness. If the hairball has become impacted in his gastro-intestinal tract, the problem is more complex. Watch your cat closely for any unusual behavior or signs he is not doing well. If the hairball is impacted, you may need to take your cat to the veterinarian to have it surgically removed.

ALL YEAR ROUND
Your indoor cat may shed for the entire year. Just accept this and make the time to comb him regularly.

HEALTHY TUMMY
Feed a complete and balanced diet to keep your cat's intestinal tract healthy.

OPEN WIDE

Check inside your cat's mouth regularly. It is best to begin massaging his teeth and gums when he is a kitten. If you notice any abnormalities, take him to the veterinarian for treatment.

WHISKERLESS CATS

Certain breeds, such as the Rex cats, cannot grow their whiskers at all. Because of the consistency of their hair, the whiskers break off close to the muzzle.

DENTAL CARE

Cats rarely get cavities but they are very susceptible to gum disease. It is important to prevent gum disease because, over the years, it can lead to bad breath, painful inflammation, receded gums, loose and infected teeth and eventually loss of teeth. It can even cause serious illness.

Have you noticed that when your veterinarian is examining your cat, she may bend down and smell the cat's breath? Mouth odor is sometimes as good a tool as a thermometer in tracking down the cause of a cat's malaise. Although mouth odor may be caused by the food the cat eats, it may also be caused by teeth that need either cleaning or extracting, gum infection or stomatitis (inflammation of the inside of the mouth). Another sign that your cat has a dental problem may be a loss of appetite. His sore gums or infected tooth can keep him from wanting to eat.

Indoor cats may be more prone to mouth problems because they do not have access to outdoor grasses (the cat's dental floss) and seldom perform the chewing action necessitated by crunching bones of small mice, birds and rabbits. Acute stomatitis may be associated with feline leukemia virus (FeLV), feline immuno-deficiency virus (FIV) and calicivirus infection (see p. 58) and chronic stomatitis may be due to dental problems. Feeding your cat dry food may assist in maintaining good dental and oral health. Preventative treatments include massaging the cat's gums and brushing his teeth (see p. 43). If problems develop, your veterinarian can make a thorough examination and treat the cat appropriately.

WHISKER PROBLEMS

Cats do not have whiskers just for looks. Whiskers are very important to your cat. He may use them as feelers to avoid bumping into things in the dark, to measure the width of a space to ensure that he will fit through, and when he is hunting.

Whiskers can also be a bother to him, especially if he tries to eat food out of a bowl. The ends of the whiskers touching the side of the bowl can transfer irritating sensations to his brain, making it hard for him to continue eating. It's rather like you eating with your head encased in a bag—the sides of the bag rubbing against your face would not make for an enjoyable meal.

Whiskers are extremely sensitive. Damage to his whiskers can cause your cat discomfort.

When he is a kitten, his mother might have chewed some or all of his whiskers off while cleaning food from them. Don't worry— this is normal and they will soon grow back.

DECLAWING

Once a kitten or cat learns to use furniture and draperies to sharpen his claws, it will be hard to convince him to stop. Start him out right by training him on a scratching post. Show him what to do by holding him near the post and scratching his claws on the surface. If you are consistent with training methods, and offer your cat a choice of objects on which to scratch, there's a good chance that you may prevent him from clawing your furniture and doing damage.

Another solution to the scratching problem is to have your cat's claws removed. Although declawing is not performed in some countries of the world, it is widely accepted in the U.S. Whether this is because more people in the U.S. live in cities and keep their cats strictly indoors has not been established.

Before you have your cat declawed, ask yourself these questions. Am I planning to keep my cat forever? Do I fully understand that he will be too vulnerable to be allowed outdoors again, unless he can be closely supervised? A declawed cat may have a hard time climbing a tree to escape a dog and cannot defend himself properly if cornered.

If you do make the decision to have your cat declawed, you should be aware that this is an orthopedic surgical procedure that calls for the removal of the claw and the first bone of each toe. Except in special cases, only the front feet should be declawed. Although your cat will be anesthetized during the surgery, it is likely that he will suffer some temporary discomfort afterward and may be reluctant to stand, walk or jump until the toes have fully healed.

TRAINING YOUR KITTENS
Encourage your kittens to use a scratching pad instead of your furniture and, if they continue to use your furniture attach orange peel to it. They dislike the smell and will quickly learn to stay away.

DECLAWING DECISION
If you decide to have your cat declawed, you should not allow him to go outdoors unsupervised.

CARING FOR AN ELDERLY CAT

✚

Your cat has been with you for many years, and you have learned to trust each other. Don't let him down now. As he enters old age, you must pay greater attention to his needs and provide plenty of tender loving care.

CARING FOR THE ELDERLY
Gently groom your aging cat every day, even if he is shorthaired. As you comb him, run your fingers lightly over his body to see if he is developing tumors. Many old-age tumors are benign, but always have a veterinarian check them.

WARM AS TOAST
It is important that you keep your aging cat warm. If you live in a cold climate, you might consider cat pajamas.

With improved diets and advances in medicine, cats, just like humans, are living longer. However, old age can vary dramatically from one cat to another. A strictly indoors cat with a good diet and regular vaccinations will probably outlive an outdoor cat, an indoor/outdoor cat and a feral cat. It is not uncommon for indoor cats to live up to 18 years or more. Outdoor cats, on the other hand, generally live to around six years, although many may die much sooner and others may live to more than 20 years.

SIGNS OF OLD AGE
You can tell if your cat is entering old age when he does not jump onto his favorite perches easily, or at all. He will sleep more, and when awake, he will move slowly and with a hint of stiffness. However, he will not be as prone to arthritis and back problems as dogs, and should remain agile for a long time.

Although you may not notice at first because he is adept at keeping to a routine, your cat may start to lose his hearing and eyesight. It's a good idea to let him see your hand in front of his face before you pick him up, and to call his name before approaching.

He may also start to develop problems with incontinence, diarrhea and constipation. Some of these are caused by kidney problems or diabetes, while others are simply part of the aging process. You will need to take him to the veterinarian to determine the cause, and then follow the prescribed treatment. If he has a constipation problem, feeding a food that contains fermentable fiber may help.

Bad breath is a sure signal to take your elderly cat to the veterinarian. It could be nothing more than a gum infection or a tooth that needs extracting, or it may signify something more serious. Don't worry if he has to have some teeth extracted. Many cats continue to eat their normal food—and even crunch dry cat food—with missing teeth.

The outdoor or aging farm cat may develop skin conditions so you will need to watch him carefully and help him maintain a clean coat.

WEIGHT AND DIET

Pay special attention to your elderly cat's weight. As he ages, he may gain or lose weight, and this could contribute to other aging problems.

Use weight trends and body condition to monitor the cat's health. Some older cats may become too thin and may require a diet that contains more nutrients and calories in each cup of food. Others, however, may tend to gain weight and require a diet lower in fat content. Old cats in reasonable body condition should be fed a high-quality diet that is easy to chew, has more than adequate protein and is lower in calories. These cats may do poorly on some lower protein "senior" diets because they need protein to keep their muscles in good condition.

EUTHANASIA

When your cat can no longer eat or drink on his own, and has lost the will to engage in his normal pastimes, it is time to think about doing the kindest thing you can for him, and that is euthanasia.

Completely outdoor cats and feral cats will remove themselves from their colony and creep off somewhere to die. However, your indoor cat doesn't have this option.

The decision to have him humanely euthanized is difficult. Not only are you contemplating the loss of your trusted friend, but you could suffer feelings of guilt. Just remember you are truly doing the right thing in putting an end to his misery and suffering in the kindest possible way. Phone-in pet loss support hotlines can connect grieving pet owners with trained professionals who can offer support during their time of mourning.

YOUR CAT'S AGE IN HUMAN YEARS

When your cat is one year old, he is a similar age to a 20-year-old human. For each year after, simply add four humans years to every one of his. For example, if he is 15 years old in cat years, he is 76 years old in human years, and may have health problems that accompany that age. Use the following chart to help you calculate the age of your cat:

CAT	HUMAN
1 year	20 years
2 years	24 years
3 years	28 years
4 years	32 years
5 years	36 years
6 years	40 years
7 years	44 years
8 years	48 years
9 years	52 years
10 years	56 years

WATCHING WEIGHT

It seems there are as many kinds of foods for cats as there are for humans, so if your aging cat is putting on weight, work out a successful diet for him with the help of your veterinarian.

FIRST AID

✚

It's easy to say that if an accident occurs, take your cat to the veterinarian.
But what if the veterinarian's office is closed? Or you live hundreds of miles
away from the veterinarian? Here are some things you'll need to know.

TRAFFIC HASSLES
Cats have no concept of the danger of the roads. Because cars do not smell like predators, cats cannot understand that they can be harmed by them. So if you live on a busy road, it is best to keep your cat indoors.

Accidents will happen, and the best way to handle them is to be prepared. Make sure you have a properly equipped first-aid kit, be aware of the types of injuries your cat might suffer, and know how best to treat them. Some treatments are straight-forward—if your cat is choking, you need to remove the obstruction from his throat. Other accidents, however, require more complex treatment, and this easy-reference section will explain how you can best treat your cat in an emergency.

BLEEDING

Although most minor bleeding will stop of its own accord, if your cat is bleeding heavily you will need to apply a pressure bandage or, in extreme cases, a tourniquet.

A pressure bandage, which stops the blood flowing at the wound, is used when the bleeding is not too severe. Apply a cold-water compress onto the wound and then put on a pressure bandage of gauze and fasten with tape or torn sheeting. The main point of bleeding will be where your cat is licking.

If your cat is bleeding profusely from a limb or a tail wound, you will need to use a tourniquet, which stops the blood flowing to the wound. To apply, bind a strip of cloth tightly above the wound. A tourniquet should be used as a last resort, and the animal must be taken immediately to the veterinarian's office.

If his paw or leg is injured and bleeding, bandage up one side and down the other and then secure it above the joint. If his tail is bleeding, wrap the bandage tightly. Never use a pin to fasten anything on a cat. Use only tape or torn sheeting.

APPLYING PRESSURE
If your cat is bleeding, apply a pressure bandage to the wound. If the bleeding continues, take him to the veterinarian for treatment.

FIRST-AID KIT

Every household should have a first-aid kit ready in case of a four-legged emergency. It should include all the items below. In addition, you will need the following items when you are away from home with your cat: carrying cage, muzzle, collar and leash, bowl for washing wounds, towel or blanket, tourniquet and sheeting for binding wounds.

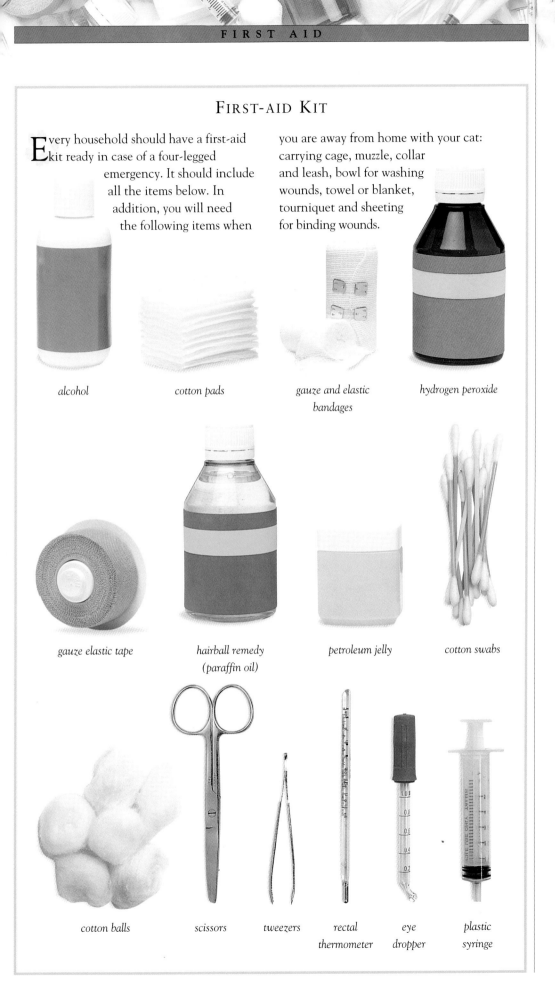

alcohol

cotton pads

gauze and elastic
bandages

hydrogen peroxide

gauze elastic tape

hairball remedy
(paraffin oil)

petroleum jelly

cotton swabs

cotton balls

scissors

tweezers

rectal
thermometer

eye
dropper

plastic
syringe

BURNS

Your cat could suffer serious injury if he jumps on a hot stove or tips over a pan of boiling water. If it is a superficial burn or scald, the affected area turns red and could blister slightly. If the burn is more serious, the skin turns white and the hairs are easily removed when pulled.

To treat minor burns, immediately apply cold water or ice to the affected area for about 20 minutes. If the burn is serious, you will need to take him to the veterinarian for further treatment.

You can help prevent these accidents by keeping pans away from the edge of the stove and by covering gas and electric rings with fireproof lids. Kitchens can be the heart of the home, and very much your cat's domain. Let him have access to this area, but take the necessary precautions.

TREATING BURNS
To treat minor burns, immediately apply ice to the area. If the burn is more serious, you need to take your cat to the veterinarian. Always remember, prevention is better than cure.

TRAUMA

If your cat has fallen from a height or is struck by a car, the most important thing to do is to prevent him from going into shock or to minimize the effects of shock. Cover him lightly, keep him warm, talk to him in low tones and a soothing manner, and do not rush. Lift him as carefully as possible so as not to worsen any damage, place him in a small container and take him to the veterinarian immediately. Only a veterinarian can treat such injuries, and often anesthesia is required.

Although you might want to try to splint a broken limb, bear in mind that most cats do not tolerate being handled when they are in pain and your best efforts will probably be greeted by teeth flashing and claws striking. You may well cause even more damage.

ELECTROCUTION

Many cats, especially kittens, will chew on wires. Some even like to chew on wire coat hangers. With today's electrical equipment, it may be almost impossible to wire-proof your house.

If your cat has been electrocuted, don't touch him until you have turned off the power and removed the plug from the socket. Check for his heartbeat by feeling the lower part of his chest just behind the left foreleg. If he is unconscious, you may need to rush him to the veterinarian for treatment. Never attempt to resuscitate him yourself.

ROUGH LANDING
Your cat will not always land on his feet, and may suffer a fracture from a bad landing. Never try to splint his leg yourself or you could both be hurt.

If the shock is not sufficient to render him senseless, it can still inflict a serious burn on his tongue or in his mouth. Take him to the veterinarian as soon as you can to avoid any possibility of gangrene.

To protect your cat from any further shocks, remember to unplug appliances when you're not using them and to keep cords out of reach.

DROWNING

Although they may be very good swimmers, cats, just like people, can drown, particularly if they fall into a swimming pool. Even a toilet bowl can be hazardous to a kitten.

If your cat is drowning, remove him from the water as quickly as possible. Then, holding him by his hind legs, swing him gently between your legs until all the water has been expelled. If he has problems breathing or acts abnormally, contact your veterinarian.

FEVER

Just like you, when your cat is sick he may have a high temperature. To take his temperature, coat a rectal thermometer with petroleum jelly. Gradually, using a slow, twisting motion, insert it about one inch (2.5 cm) into his rectum, and hold it in place for a few minutes. Do not jam or force the thermometer into the rectum.

If your cat is running a fever, take him to the veterinarian immediately.

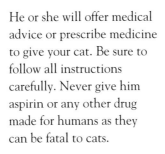

He or she will offer medical advice or prescribe medicine to give your cat. Be sure to follow all instructions carefully. Never give him aspirin or any other drug made for humans as they can be fatal to cats.

SAVING LIVES

To revive your cat if he is drowning, swing him between your legs. Continue to do so until the water in his lungs gushes outward, and it has all been expelled.

TAKING HIS TEMPERATURE

When taking your cat's temperature, use a rectal thermometer. A cat's normal temperature is 101°F (38°C) with certain breeds (the Rex and the Sphynx) having normal temperatures of 102–103°F (39–39.5°C). Take your cat to the veterinarian if his reading is 2° or more above normal.

POISONING

Most household products that are poisonous to humans will also be poisonous to your cat. Make sure you keep all your cleaners and other such substances well out of harm's way. Even anti-freeze could be fatal to your cat if he licks drops of it from underneath the car. If you think your cat has been poisoned, contact your veterinarian immediately. He or she can offer instructions to induce vomiting.

VOMITING

It is not unusual for your cat to vomit, and he may be doing nothing more than ridding himself of a hairball (see p. 73). Similarly, if your cat is vomiting only after meals, he may simply be overeating. Try putting a smaller amount of food in his bowl. Or if yours is a multi-cat household, make sure he has his own food bowl. Your cats may be competing for food and therefore eating too quickly.

If vomiting continues, see your veterinarian. Vomiting

clematis

yew

poinsettia

delphinium

POISONOUS PLANTS

The indoor cat is exposed to just about as many toxic substances as the outdoor one. We often forget that the thriving philodendron plant or blooming wisteria can be toxic to him, so here is a list of some of the common plants that are potentially dangerous to your cat.

Anemone	Elephant's Ear	Larkspur
Azalea	English Ivy	Liburnum
Black Cherry	Foxglove	Lily-of-the-valley
Bloodroot	Four o'Clock	Lupin
Buttercup	Hellebore	Mistletoe
Caladium	Hemlock	Morning Glory
Castor Bean	Holly	Mountain Laurel
Clematis	Hyacinth	Oleander
Crocus	Hydrangea	Philodendron
Cycad	Indian Spurge Tree	Poinciana
Daphne	Jack-in-the-pulpit	Poinsettia
Delphinium	Jerusalem Cherry	Poison Ivy
Dicentra	Jimson Weed	Poison Oak
Dieffenbachia	Lantana	Pokeweed
		Rhododendron
		Solandra
		Star of Bethlehem
		Sweet Pea
		Thornapple
		Wisteria
		Yew

DINNER FOR TWO

When your cats are sharing the same food dish, they will often compete for the contents and eat very quickly. If this is causing any of them to vomit, try encouraging them to eat more slowly by giving them each their own dish in their own special place.

may be a sign of many illnesses. You may want to stop feeding him for 12 hours, but give plenty of water to drink to avoid dehydration. Then give him only bland foods (available from your veterinarian) for the next 24 hours. If everything seems fine, slowly reintroduce variety into his diet.

Whenever your cat's vomiting is combined with not eating, not drinking, or not behaving in his usual manner, or if there are signs of blood in his vomit, you should take him straight to the veterinarian. This could signal one of many more serious illnesses, including poisoning, gastritis, ulcers or even feline infectious enteritis (FIE) (see p. 58).

UP IN A TREE

One day you may find your cat stuck in a tree, and neither one of you will know what to do. In most cases, when he feels hungry, he will find his own way down. But sometimes, if he is sick or panicked, he will be too frightened to come down and you will need to step in. Try calling and coaxing him into reach with his favorite food, treat or toy. Call your local fire department if you need additional assistance.

If all these methods fail, then it's time for more drastic measures—climbing the tree. Cover yourself with a long-sleeved shirt and wear thick gloves for your hands (he will probably scratch and may even try to bite you). Take along a small towel; if you can cover him with that you have a better chance of catching him. You will need to stay very calm because if he becomes any more frightened, he may climb even higher up the tree.

If all attempts at rescue fail, all you can do is leave his favorite food as close to him as possible. Be sure to check on him every so often to help him down if he needs assistance.

BACK TO EARTH

If you have been unable to remove your cat from the tree, see if you can tempt him down by offering him some of his favorite food.

BREEDING AND SHOWING

A kitten is so flexible that she is almost double; the hind parts are equivalent to another kitten with which the forepart plays. She does not discover that her tail belongs to her until you tread upon it.

HENRY DAVID THOREAU (1817-1862),
American essayist, naturalist and poet

THE BREEDING CYCLE

The excitement of breeding a cat to meet its standard is addictive and can last for a lifetime. Be warned, though, that very few, if any, breeders actually make a profit.

When a female cat, or queen, is ready to mate, she is said to be in season, in estrus or in heat. When she comes in season, she will emit loud cries, or calls, to attract a tomcat. She will also crouch down and creep about the floor on shortened legs, and may even spray.

As her season progresses she will rub against you or an article of furniture, raise her rear end into the air and make alluring little noises. You may also notice that her vulva is swollen and some clear discharge may be visible.

COMING IN SEASON
As with this female, there are usually clearly visible signs when your queen is in season and ready to mate.

FREQUENCY OF SEASONS
Although the outdoor queen may come in season in spring and again in early fall if the weather turns clement, the indoor queen may cycle in and out of season every few weeks throughout the entire year until she is bred. This is because of the more or less constant temperature in the home or cattery and the artificial light (similar to the sun in spring and summer).

Frequent seasons pose dangers for your queen. Many females will not eat when in season and can become dangerously thin. They also have a greater chance of developing pyometra, (see p. 64).

Frequent seasons can also present a problem for your queen if she already has a litter of kittens and should not be bred for some time. Yes, she will come in season even while she is nursing and very often when the kittens are as young as three weeks. Another pregnancy at this early stage may really wear her down.

If you don't want your queen to fall pregnant at a particular time, but want her to remain intact for future breeding, you must either confine her or the studcat so they cannot gain access to each other.

You can also try to induce ovulation in the queen which may take her out of season in a few days instead of one week. Apply petroleum jelly to the end of a clean rectal thermometer and gently insert it into her vagina. Twist it slowly and gently and

she should soon let out a shriek. This is a sure sign you have achieved the same result as a tomcat. Immediately withdraw the thermometer and then repeat the procedure ten minutes later and again later that day.

THE MATING RITUAL

When the female is fully in season and ready to accept the male (she and the male work this out themselves and there is nothing you can do to hasten the process), she will flirt with him, rub her cheek on the floor and then offer him her backside, holding her tail to one side. He will jump on her and grab the back of her neck with his teeth. This usually subdues

her and she will submit. He then straddles her and proceeds to enter her from the rear. He breeds her quickly and, when penetration is achieved, she will let loose with a blood-curdling shriek. The wise male will hurry to remove himself from her proximity before she turns and strikes out at him with her claws. Once he is out of her reach, she proceeds to roll about on the floor for several minutes, making noises.

When she has finished rolling, she will sit up and clean herself thoroughly, preparing herself for a repeat performance. Within about ten minutes, she is back at him again with her coy little noises, head rubbing and flirtatious ways. He will again respond as before and the process repeats, complete with another shriek on her part.

MATING FOR PREGNANCY

To achieve pregnancy, it is generally best to allow cats to mate over one or two days, although this will depend on the individual cats. Whereas some males and females can be left together and enjoy each other's company, others will need to be separated as they can turn on each other and fight between matings.

INTERMISSION

After mating, the queen will roll about and clean herself. She will then, in a very short space of time, be ready to mate again and will start flirting with the tomcat.

LITTER SIZE

Although there is no way to plan the size of a litter, there are on average three or four kittens per litter, as with these Balinese.

LITTER, SEX AND NUMBERS

There is no truth to the notion that breeding your queen either early or late in her season will result in her having fewer kittens. There is also no truth to the idea that you can dictate how many males and females she will have by breeding on a certain day of her season. The male determines the sex and the female determines the number in the litter. You might breed her in the middle of a heavy season, and she will conceive just one kitten. Or she might escape from her cage and have the male mate with her just once and she will conceive eight kittens. However, a litter will generally average three or four kittens.

CHOOSING A MATE

Before you consider breeding cats, ask yourself if you are willing to sit up all night with an expectant queen, or to give up your annual vacation because you cannot leave a house full of cats!

THE STUD HIMSELF
The studcat's owner should provide you with a five-generation pedigree, but a minimum of three generations is acceptable if you do not plan to show.

Unless you are breeding purebred cats for a specific purpose, it is not recommended that you breed cats. You will simply be adding to the unwanted kitten population.

WHAT TO LOOK FOR

When selecting the ideal partner for your queen, ask to see his pedigree, or family tree. In addition to the colors of his ancestors listed on the chart, ask if his owner knows the colors of his litter mates. These cats do not appear on the pedigree but can affect the colors of the kittens your female will produce. For instance, the pedigree might simply show the seal points, but two seal points can produce a blue point if their litter mates or their ancestors' litter mates are blue points.

Many breeders choose a studcat based on the number of champions and grand champions in his pedigree. For one reason or another many cats may not have been shown, yet their bloodlines may be identical to others who have been shown. The bloodline is what's important, and the traits and health information carried in certain bloodlines is what you should look for.

You will also need to select a male to complement your female. If she has a long tail and her standard calls for a short tail, choose a male with a short tail. Remember, however, that inheritance of many traits is complex.

CLEAN AND HEALTHY

It is important to find a studcat who comes from healthy stock and is in good health. Make sure that your queen and the studcat are current on their vaccinations.

You must take your female to the studcat. He does not come to you. So be sure to visit the quarters where the studcat is housed. In many cases, this will be a large cage in someone's home or a cage in a shed or garage. Check that his bedding, litter pan and general surroundings are clean. You can expect to find a strong odor in his quarters. The studcat's urine, both in his litter pan and where he has sprayed, is strong. This does not mean that he is unclean—no amount of cleaning will take away that strong odor.

Make sure his quarters are free from drafts and climate-controlled. Check with his owner if she is present while the breeding is going on to ensure the stud doesn't hurt the queen, or vice versa. The ethical breeder will witness the matings. The unethical one will tell you they think a mating took place, and this will leave you wondering for a few weeks before you know if your queen is pregnant or not. It is vital for the breeder to be able to tell you that the cats have definitely mated.

SETTLING IN

Even if your queen is in season and howling for a male, don't be surprised if she goes out of season as soon as she arrives at the studcat's home. Very often either the trip or the stress of being in a strange place will put her out of season. The queen should not immediately be put in with the male, whether she is in or out of season. She should be placed in a cage next to his. Sometimes she will hiss and spit at him and hide in the bed in her cage. If she doesn't go out of season, she will usually relax and start to rub herself against the bars of the cage nearest his. That is when the breeder can place her in the cage with the male. If she does nothing but curl up and hiss and growl, you may be asked to take her home and try another time.

If you have sent your female by airplane for the mating, and she goes out of season from the stress of the trip, the breeder may keep her for a few weeks until she comes back in season and can be bred.

THE STUD HOUSE
Before sending your queen to the studcat for mating, settle the cost of the stud service and find out whether a free repeat breeding will be offered in the event she either doesn't conceive or has a litter consisting of only one kitten.

ODD ONE OUT
It is important when choosing a studcat that you check that his litter mates all have the characteristics you are trying to achieve: ear shape, for example, or coat color. Otherwise, as with this litter of Scottish Folds, you might not get everything you expected.

THE PREGNANCY

Be aware of your queen's needs and try to make her pregnancy as easy as possible. Although her behavior may change significantly during this time, this is perfectly natural and not a cause for concern.

When your cat becomes pregnant, you'll notice many changes in her, from her temperament to her appetite. Even though this time may be difficult for both of you, it is important that you take proper precautions so she and her kittens are happy and healthy. Try to avoid taking your queen anywhere during her pregnancy. Handle her gently, and do not let anyone carry her roughly.

At about three weeks, turn her over on her back and look at her nipples. They should be turning pink in color and starting to enlarge. You will also notice at this point that she has become swollen around her vulva; this is more easily seen on shorthaired or light-colored queens.

TEMPERAMENT CHANGES
Your pregnant queen's temperament may change—for better or for worse. Hormonal changes may result in her not wanting other cats near her. She may even go so far as to attack one of her favorite companions. This is natural behavior, so don't punish her. It may be best to confine her to a room or confine the other pets until this phase passes.

As she progresses through her pregnancy, her temperament will probably change yet again and she may actually seek out other cats. She'll want to

CHECKING FOR PREGNANCY
A veterinarian or experienced breeder may be able to confirm pregnancy.

A DAILY CLEANSE
During the last few weeks of your queen's pregnancy you may need to gently clean the area around her anus with a soft cloth and water. As with this Maine Coon, the increasing girth of her stomach sometimes makes it difficult for her to reach around to clean herself properly.

cuddle up to them and she will even allow them to nurse on her. She is in full maternal bloom. Don't be surprised if she picks up a soft toy in her mouth and carries it about the house, mewing softly. This is her make-believe kitten and she is practicing being a mother.

She'll also be inclined to show you more affection, and may expect you to show her more attention, too. As her tummy increases in girth, she may flop on her back to have you gently stroke her abdomen. She'll fall asleep purring while you stroke.

APPETITE CHANGES
Although your queen is supposed to eat more while pregnant, some queens don't experience an increase in appetite. If she is otherwise in good health, do not worry. Make sure she is eating a high-quality diet that has been tested to meet the needs of cats for gestation (pregnancy), lactation (milk production) and growth.

KEEP A CLOSE EYE
Watch closely throughout your queen's pregnancy for signs of illness or listlessness. If you spot these signs, take her to the veterinarian as she could be suffering from a uterine infection or false pregnancy, or she could be having a miscarriage. Make sure you record the exact date that she was bred as this is vital information for your veterinarian in determining the possible causes of her ailments. It is also important for you to know this in order to prepare for the birth and to be on hand when she delivers. A cat will generally carry kittens for 63 days, although she can have them as early as 58 or 59 days and as late as 67 or 68 days with no ill effects. Any period of time shorter or longer generally indicates trouble, and you should contact the veterinarian.

DELIVERY ROOM
Prepare a place for your queen to deliver her kittens in good time. If she is a cattery cat, then her cage will be fine, but if she is your house cat, a low drawer pulled halfway out of a dresser and lined with soft cloth may be suitable. A box placed on the floor of a closet with the door ajar is also a good site. She is generally happy for you to select the area.

PREGNANT PAUSE
Your queen is at the mercy of her hormones, and her behavior may change accordingly. Pregnant cats may be unusually content and affectionate.

OUTDOOR CAT
If the queen is an outdoor cat, provide her with a refuge where both she and her kittens will feel safe and where they will be undisturbed by curious visitors.

THE BIRTH

Watching your queen give birth is one of the most satisfying parts of breeding. Although she will rarely need assistance, your queen will appreciate your presence, particularly if anything should go wrong. Just remember that too much human meddling may be deleterious.

When your queen is approaching her 59th day of pregnancy, you should confine her to the cage or room in which she is to deliver her kittens.

She may fool you into thinking that birth is imminent by scratching and tearing at the paper or toweling in the birthing box, becoming very restless and not wanting much to eat. However, these signs can go on for one to two weeks and are not sure-fire indicators of labor. In fact, in some cases these signs may have started to occur at the time she was mated.

Her temperature will drop to below 101.2°F (38.4°C) for a 24-hour period before delivery, although it is not

THE BIRTHING PROCESS
It is unusual for your queen to have much difficulty when giving birth. Even with her first litter, a queen knows instinctively what to do.

DELIVERING
The queen delivers her first kitten within about 15 minutes of the onset of labor. Depending on the number of kittens, labor will last for up to two or three hours.

CLEANING
After giving birth, the queen will chew off the umbilical cord and eat the placenta. In the wild, the placenta would attract predators, so this behavior is vital. She will then lick her kittens clean.

advisable to take her temperature at this time as this could stress her. Other definitive signs are a tightening of the skin over her abdomen and the movement, or dropping, of the kittens to the rear. She will meow quite plaintively during this time, but she may have been doing this during most of her pregnancy.

LABOR

Be alert to any signs that labor has begun. You will notice her squatting and straining and, if she is shorthaired, you may also see labor contractions rippling. If she is longhaired, you will have cut away the hair from around her

vagina so the hair doesn't stick to the umbilical cord during delivery. You also should have cut the hair from around her nipples to enable the kittens to suck on them more easily. If she is shorthaired, these procedures are not necessary.

THE BIRTH

You will usually see a mucus discharge from the vaginal opening, which indicates that birth is imminent. You should be on hand to comfort her but do not be too hasty about stepping in to help. You may do more harm than good.

The queen should deliver the first kitten within 15 minutes of her first beginning to

BIRTHING CHECKLIST

When preparing for a home birth, make sure that you have the following items on hand:

- Hand towels
- Kitchen towels
- Sterilized scissors
- Heating pad/hot water bottle
- Clean bedding
- Garbage bags

NURSING

Soon after being born, the kittens will shakily make their way around to their mother's nipples and start feeding.

MOTHER CARE

The queen will feed and clean her kittens, and eat their urine and excrement until they are able to use a litter pan—usually at about three weeks of age.

A CLOSER LOOK
Closely inspect the newborn kittens to check that they are properly formed. Be very careful not to cause them any unnecessary harm or anxiety.

crouch, strain and cry, and she will purr throughout the entire delivery. The remaining kittens will be delivered at intervals of between 5 and 30 minutes.

If the kitten is delivered head first, the queen should need no help. If it is delivered hind feet first (breech birth) and it does not arrive for five minutes or so, you will need to assist. Make sure your hands are clean, wrap a soft towel around the kitten's body and gently manipulate him, trying to coordinate with the mother's contractions, if possible. Do not pull on the tail or the legs or they may come off in your hands. Do not squeeze the abdomen, either.

If labor continues and no kittens appear for more than an hour, or if a kitten or two have been born and labor goes on for another hour or so without another kitten

appearing, then you should call the veterinarian. He will instruct you as to the best course of action; this might involve taking your queen into his office so that he can assist. If you allow labor to go on too long without kittens appearing, you risk not only having the kittens die but also possibly losing your queen.

THE FIRST BREATH
After giving birth, most queens will immediately open the sacs over the kittens' faces so that they can take their first breath. If this is your queen's first litter and she is struggling, or if she doesn't do this straight away, you should tear open the sacs for her with your nails. Then place each kitten near the queen's mouth so that she can stimulate the kittens' breathing by licking them.

If any of the kittens appear to be in distress, you should dry them and keep them warm. You should consult your veterinarian if the kitten does not nurse.

FEEDING TIME
The queen, as with this Abyssinian, will nurse her kittens until they are about three weeks of age. At this time they will start eating semi-solid and solid foods, but may still nurse occasionally for several weeks.

Most queens will chew off the umbilical cord and then eat the placenta. Give her 15 minutes or so to perform this chore. If she still hasn't cut the cord by this time, then you can do so by tying a piece of string around the umbilical cord about 1 inch (2.5 cm) from the kitten's stomach. Then, using sterilized scissors, cut the cord on the outside of the string, farthest from the kitten's stomach. Or, using your fingernails, clamp the cord tightly, and using a scissor motion, cut back and forth, until the cord has been severed. Then, with the sterilized scissors, cut the cord, again about one inch (2.5 cm) from the kitten's abdomen.

The queen will generally eat the placenta and excess umbilical cord. She has an instinctive fear that predators will be attracted by them and will harm the newborn kittens. Even the completely domesticated queen has these instincts, passed down to her through generations of ancestors who lived in the wild.

The queen will then wash her kittens, and at this stage you may want to weigh the newborn kittens.

POST-BIRTH

Some veterinarians advise giving your queen a shot of oxytocin within 12 hours of giving birth. This shot may be dispensed for you to administer at home, or you may need to take your queen to the veterinarian for it. This shot is given to make sure that no remnants of the placenta are left in the uterus

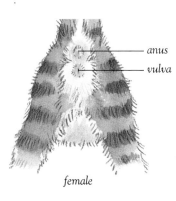

female

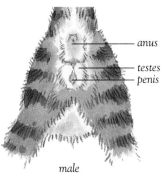

male

where they might cause infection. It is also helpful in inducing the milk supply. Your veterinarian may also recommend that the queen be put on an antibiotic for seven to ten days after the kittens are born to help ward off any minor infections the kittens might catch while nursing.

Provide your queen with clean bedding, and make sure she and the kittens are housed in dim lighting, away from any drafts and the hustle and bustle of the household. The room temperature should be kept at 70°F (21°C). If this is not possible and the room is too cold, then an infrared heating light or a heating pad placed under the toweling is recommended. If, on the other hand, the room is too hot, the queen will separate herself from the kittens to cool them down.

Always place her food, water and litter pan within easy reach as the queen will not want to leave her kittens. Lactating queens have high nutrient needs, so give her all she will eat of a high-quality cat food.

DETERMINING SEX
You can determine the sex of each kitten by simply lifting up its tail and checking against the drawings above.

MOVING AROUND
The queen will always pick up her very small kittens by the scruff of their neck but they grow up quickly and soon she won't be able to lift them this way.

WARM AS TOAST

Kittens will keep warm by snuggling up together with the queen. In cooler climates, you may want to give them some extra warmth by providing them with a heated cat bed.

GROWTH STAGES

Between seven and ten days, the kittens will start to open their eyes (left). At three weeks they will be more alert and ready to eat semi-solid food, and they will start using the litter pan (center left). By six weeks, they will become more playful (center right) and by 11 weeks they should be well on their way to settling into their new homes (right).

NEWBORN KITTENS

When the kittens are between seven and ten days old, their eyes should open. If they don't, gently blot them with cotton balls dipped in warm water until they do. Very often, the opening of the eyes will be accompanied by creamy-looking matter, which should be gently cleaned away. Eye infections can be common in kittens, so check the eyes often, administer any eye ointment your veterinarian may have prescribed and repeat the bathing process regularly.

Aside from changing the queen's bedding, feeding her and making sure the kittens' eyes are clean, there is very little to do for the next two to three weeks. It is a good idea to pick the kittens up every day, turn them over on their backs and stroke their stomachs. This not only accustoms them to being handled but is also an opportunity to check their health. By holding the kittens up to your face you can tell if they smell. The healthy kitten will have absolutely no odor, while the kitten with a health problem will.

CLEANING AND FEEDING

The mother will clean the kittens and consume their urine and excrement until the kittens start using the litter pan. This usually happens when they are introduced to semi-solid food at three to four weeks of age, although this will vary depending on the kittens' health and size, and on whether the mother still has a good supply of milk. Feed weaning kittens a good-quality dry kitten food moistened with water.

ORPHAN KITTENS

If the worst happens and your queen dies during delivery, or if she has a Cesarean section to aid in delivery, you may have to become the kittens' mother, and you will need to take extra care. Orphan kittens need an additional source of heat, such as a heating pad or infrared lamp, and must be kept away from drafts.

FEEDING
ORPHAN KITTENS

The kittens will be deprived of colostrum (first milk), which contains many valuable nutrients and antibodies that protect the kittens until they are weaned. You can obtain

kitten milk formulas from your veterinarian or a pet store, but these do not contain all the nutrients or antibodies of their mother's milk. Make sure that the formula is at room temperature and give them only a few drops at a time as their stomachs are very small—follow the manufacturer's guidelines.

For the first week of their lives, the kittens will need to be fed every two hours. After each feeding, take a soft cloth and gently wipe against the genitals and rectum to stimulate them to excrete. You will also need to wash their faces and bottoms. As the kittens eat more, you can increase the amount of time between feedings.

DEVELOPING KITTENS

You do not need to take the queen away from the kittens as she will naturally discourage them from nursing when she sees fit. They will start to sample adult food at about three weeks of age, and will probably eat a total of several ounces (100 grams) each, spread over the course of the day. If they are not eating by themselves by four weeks, you can help the weaning process by smearing food on your fingers and letting the kittens lick them, gradually moving the fingers to a saucer of food. You can also offer them moistened dry food. This will help them adapt to dry food when fully weaned. Make sure the queen does not eat their food.

As soon as the kittens start to eat solid food, ensure that a litter pan is placed nearby. They will quickly learn to use it naturally by watching their mother.

Although you have handled them gently for the first three weeks of their lives, once they start walking around you can initiate gentle play by trailing a ribbon for them to follow. Their eyes are not well focused at this age, and they're not coordinated, so don't expect too much of them. Also, don't place them on high surfaces until they are older and can recognize the dangers, as they can easily fall.

At six weeks, the kittens become very active and after their first vaccination, usually at eight weeks, most are ready for their new homes.

FEEDING ORPHANS

Try feeding orphan kittens with nursing bottles made especially for kittens. If this doesn't work, try using a syringe or an eye dropper.

AN INTRODUCTION TO SHOWING

Although plenty of hard work goes into preparing your cat for the show ring, this should also be lots of fun. And the thrill of having her shown and win a ribbon makes it all worthwhile.

THE NEWCOMERS
The first visit to a cat show can be somewhat overwhelming for both you and your cat. Don't be concerned though as it won't be long before you realize how enjoyable it can be.

All cats must be healthy and free from ticks, lice, ringworm, fleas and any other parasites in order to be shown. If your cat has been exposed to a contagious disease within 21 days of the show, then she is not eligible to be shown. You must also ensure that she is current on her vaccinations, and it is sometimes helpful to give the show cat more frequent booster shots, but check this with your veterinarian. Shows in the U.S. no longer demand a veterinary inspection of your cat before she is admitted to the show hall, but shows held in other countries do—each cat is examined by a veterinarian and certified free of disease and/or external parasites.

GROOMING FOR SHOWING
Your cat should be bathed before a show. Clip her nails prior to bathing, and be sure to clean her ears. Although a shorthaired cat needs only a quick brush and her coat slicked down with your hand or a chamois, a longhaired cat requires a lot more effort.

The longhaired cat cannot wait until show time for her bath. If she is being shown on a regular basis, she must be bathed weekly and combed twice daily. This will avoid mats and tangles, lessen shedding and promote a healthier coat.

You will also learn some of the grooming tricks over time. For example, to modify the appearance of large ears, you

GETTING READY
Once you have been to a few shows, and learned many of the grooming tricks, you'll be able to present your cat as attractively as this Himalayan.

THE FINISHING TOUCHES
Before taking your cat to the ring for judging, be sure to make the final touches to her coat to ensure that she is presented at her absolute best.

WHAT TO TAKE WITH YOU

- Small litter pan
- Food dish
- Water dish
- Comb
- Brush
- Cotton swabs
- Powder (cornstarch, talcum powder or fuller's earth)
- Paper towels
- Cat food
- Cat toys
- Cage curtains (to cover back, two sides and top of cage)
- Rug or towel for base of cage
- Bed
- Garbage bags (for litter)
- Food and beverages (for you)

will learn to fluff up the hair on the top of her head. To make her tail appear shorter, you will learn to trim the excess hair at the end of the tail. To make her neck look thicker and shorter, comb out her ruff so that it stands out to frame her face. Some professionals cut the hair over the eyes to make the eyes look rounder, and clip the hair around the face to give it a rounded look. When preparing her for the show, you may want to consult with professionals and breeders.

ENTERING YOUR CAT

Every association in every country will have different rules for entering a cat in a show. However, to be eligible for showing, most associations require that all cats over the age of eight months are registered.

Generally, you must enter your cat in a show at least four weeks in advance. Fill out an entry form obtained from the entry clerk and send it back with the fee. Some clubs will accept entries the week before the show, but it is best to enter early, as most shows have a limit on the number of cats they will accept.

CLASSES

In the U.S. the kitten class is for kittens four to eight months of age. If your cat is over eight months of age, she will compete as an adult in the open class. She must take a certain number of winner ribbons, or points, to gain the title Champion. After she has been shown as a Champion, she must again earn a certain number of points to become Grand Champion. There are seven registries in North America with differing requirements for showing, so check with the one in your area. Some associations offer further titles of Master Grand Champion and Supreme Grand Champion. Household pets can also earn the same titles on a similar point system to purebred cats.

The shows also offer classes for neutered or spayed cats. Adult neuters and spays are shown in the altered class, while kittens four to eight months of age that are neutered or spayed are still shown in the kitten class. The altered class offers titles of Champion, Grand Champion and Master Grand Champion. Kitten classes do not offer titles.

A MIXED VARIETY
Cats don't have to be purebred to be beautiful. Many associations allow mixed breeds, or household pets, to be shown as well as purebred cats.

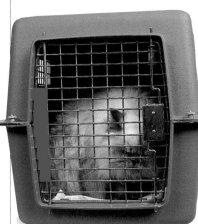

ON THE ROAD
Even though you will be given a cage for your cat when you arrive at the show, you should always take her there in a carrying case.

THE JUDGING RING
In the U.S., the judge will take the cat out of her cage, place her on the table, and then examine her against the standards of the breed.

THE SHOW BEGINS
When you arrive, you will be given a cage for your cat with an entry number attached, as well as a show catalog. The catalog lists the entrants' names and vital statistics as well as the classes in which the cats are entered. Be sure to check that all the information on your cat is accurate. If you should find an error, contact the show management immediately to have a correction made. Failure to do so may result in the voiding of wins or points that your cat may earn. The catalog will also contain a schedule detailing the order in which each judging ring will be judging the different classes.

U.S. SHOWS
In the U.S., judging is conducted in a manner far different from that of other countries. The owner carries her cat to the judging ring and places her in a judging cage. Chairs are provided in each ring so that you may sit and watch your cat being judged. Try to keep talking to a minimum because it can be distracting to a judge. Also, too many loud voices can upset a cat, who may already be frightened by being handled by a stranger with strange cats all around.

Some shows in the U.S. will have between four and twelve judging rings at a time with each cat being judged separately by four to twelve judges. Each judge conducts "her own" show. The first judge takes the cat out of the cage, sets it on the judging table and examines it

thoroughly. The judge will check for muscle tone, obesity, muscle development, coat texture, sex of the cat (if unaltered), eye shape, skull formation under the fur, ear set, boning in the legs, length of tail, shape of feet and soundness of the coat. She then returns the cat to the judging cage and washes her hands and the judging table with a disinfectant. She records any comments or awards to be given in the judging book, and hangs the appropriate ribbon, if any, on the cat's cage. Each cat is similarly judged by the other judges in the ring who, in turn, hang the appropriate ribbon, if any, on the cage.

Each cat competes within its own sex and color class and then competes for Best of Breed. Ultimately, each judge will select ten cats (unaltered, altered or kittens) for her top ten Best-in-Show awards.

The numbers for the cats so chosen are placed on top of the judging cages and the owners place their cats in the appropriate cages. The judge normally takes each cat out of the cage and presents it to the audience, listing its attributes. She then returns it to the cage and hangs the corresponding ribbons on the cage, for example Tenth Best Cat. This procedure is followed until the Best Cat is proudly displayed.

After your cat has been judged and, if successful, a ribbon hung on her cage, the ring clerk will let you know when to return her to her exhibition cage.

Pay attention to the loud speaker as there is a chance that your cat will be called back for tie-breakers or even for a final award.

INTERNATIONAL SHOWS
There are two methods of judging cats outside of the U.S. One is to have an appointed steward bring one cat at a time to the judge, who is seated behind a table. The judge examines and evaluates the cat, and writes up comments on a preprinted form, listing its good and bad points. The steward then returns the cat to its owner and repeats the process for the other cats. The judge does not hang any award ribbons; that is done by the club officials. After all judging is completed, the panel of judges votes on each group of cats and selects the best out of each group, culminating in an ultimate vote for Best Cat in Show. Unfortunately, unlike the open ring judging in the U.S., the exhibitors are not close enough to observe the process.

The other method of judging is to provide the judge with a waist-high rolling table upon which there is room to place a cat as well as a sponge and a bowl of disinfectant. The judge is accompanied by a steward who assists her as she rolls the table from cage to cage and examines the cats in order. The exhibitors are not allowed in the show hall while the judging is in progress, but are granted admittance when it is completed and the awards have been hung on the cages.

Even if your cat doesn't receive a final award, remember that the cat fancy is a hobby and a hobby should be fun. So enjoy the day, meet new friends and exchange good ideas for grooming, and you'll go home feeling like a winner.

INTERNATIONAL SHOW
In international shows, the owners of the cats will not be able to watch the judging process. The steward will take the cat to the table for judging.

A GREAT DAY OUT
Like this Norwegian Forest Cat, your cat can earn points and titles in her own class. She is also eligible to win an award for Best Cat in Show.

THE HISTORY OF THE CAT

Of all God's creatures there is only one that cannot be made the slave of the lash. That one is the cat. If man could be crossed with the cat it would improve man, but it would deteriorate the cat.

MARK TWAIN (1835-1910),
American writer and humorist

THE CAT AND ITS RELATIVES

The cat family can trace its history back 35 million years. Since then, many new species have emerged that have all shared certain "catlike" traits. Today, there are 36 species of these amazing carnivores, including the domestic cat.

OPEN WIDE

Pseudailurus gave rise to saber-toothed cats, such as *Smilodon fatalis* (right) of North America, which lived until about 10,000 years ago.

BACK IN TIME

The tiger is part of the cat family Felidae. This big cat evolved from an ancestor not much larger than a house cat.

If you traveled back in time, to a forest of 35 million years ago, you would instantly recognize a *Proailurus* stalking along a branch as a cat. An unusual breed, perhaps, but clearly a cat. *Proailurus* is the cat from which all extinct and living cats of the family Felidae are believed to have arisen, and even that long ago, the traits that make all cats superb predators were in place—stabbing teeth, powerful jaws, flesh-ripping claws, agile bodies with flexible limbs and excellent binocular vision.

Proailurus appeared at a time of great evolutionary activity, in which today's carnivore families evolved from a group of creatures called miacids. Miacids probably most resembled today's catlike civets and genets. They diversified into two subgroups of carnivores— the New World branch comprising bears, dogs, raccoons, weasels, seals and sea lions, and the Old World branch consisting of cats, hyenas, mongooses and civets.

The 36 living cat species, from 600-pound (270 kg) tigers to 2.5-pound (1 kg) black-footed cats, share an ancestor that is similar to an

JAGUAR EATING TURTLE
Jaguars, part of the Panthera lineage of cats, are unique in that they enjoy a steady diet of turtles.

BIRD'S-EYE VIEW
Native to South America, margays are part of the Ocelot lineage. They are great climbers and rarely leave the trees.

ocelot, called *Pseudailurus*, a descendent of *Proailurus*, that lived in Eurasia between 10 and 15 million years ago. From this ancestor, cats diversified and spread throughout the world, leaving only Australia and Antarctica without native cats.

Cats were among the most successful of all mammals in colonizing the earth. Lions once occupied a larger area than any other mammal, from parts of South America, through North America, Asia, Europe and Africa. Wild cats, the ancestors of domestic cats, found homes from the southern tip of Africa to the farthest reaches of Europe and Asia. In the last 10,000 years, however, these magnificent predators have steadily lost ground to their only serious competitors—people—and we could see many species of cat become extinct in our lifetime.

THE CAT FAMILY
Until recently, the cat family, Felidae, was classified into three groups based on their similarities and differences: Big cats (*Panthera*) were grouped together because they are big and kill big prey; small cats (*Felis*) were grouped together because they are

relatively small and usually take small prey, although pumas, long included in this group, are quite big and take large prey; and cheetahs (*Acinonyx*), with their lanky bodies, retractable but unsheathed claws, and adaptations for high speed, formed their own group.

However, species can look very much alike not because they are closely related but because they are adapted to similar lifestyles. So, by studying the genetic make-up of the cat family scientists have reclassified them into eight groups, called lineages. The cats within each lineage are more closely related to each other than to the cats in other lineages. The Panthera lineage consists of the six species of big cats—lions, tigers, jaguars, leopards, snow leopards and clouded leopards. The Ocelot lineage is made up of seven small South American

A SOLITARY LIFE
Pumas, or mountain lions, are solitary animals, living and hunting on their own. They cover large areas of land, from snow-covered mountains to tropical forests, hunting their prey.

SNOW LEOPARD

The snow leopard is part of the Panthera lineage. Although it is a large cat, it neither roars as other big cats do nor purrs as most small cats do.

DINNER FOR ONE

Leopards are extremely strong animals. They hunt prey and carry it up into the trees where they can eat it and rest without intrusion.

cats—ocelots, margays, oncillas, pampas cats, Andean mountain cats, kod kod and Geoffrey's cats. Then there is the Lynx lineage of lynxes, bobcats, and more surprisingly the marbled cats of Asia, which, based on distribution, habits and physical appearance, were long thought to be a type of miniature clouded leopard.

The African caracal, with beautiful tufted ears, and the African golden cat form the Caracal lineage, while the latter's look-alike, the Asian golden cat is allied with the little-known Bornean bay cat in the Bay Cat lineage. Asia's fishing cats and flat-headed cats, both unusual in their ability to catch fish, the common leopard cat and the rare Iriomote cat, found only on the Pacific island of the same name, make up the Asian Leopard Cat lineage. Most surprising is the Puma lineage, which consists of that big "small cat" as well as the slinky jaguarundi and the cheetah. Two species remain unclassified, the lanky, big-eared African serval, which specializes in pouncing on rodents as they emerge from underground burrows, and the rusty-spotted cat, a native of India and Sri Lanka that

at under three pounds rivals the black-footed cat for the title of world's smallest cat.

Finally, there is the Domestic Cat lineage, which groups your favorite pet and its wild ancestors with the tiny black-footed cat, the desert-dwelling sand cat, the long-furred, flat-faced Pallas cat of Asia, the plain-coated jungle cat and the rare Chinese mountain cat.

BIG CATS

Although genetic analysis has exposed the secrets of the cat relatives, it says little about how cats live and what they do. In fact, ecologists still find dividing cats along size lines—small, medium and large—most useful. Lions and tigers, virtual twins under the skin and far larger than the other big cats, are also similar in their total dependence on large prey. These cats are simply too big to survive on the

A FAMILY AFFAIR
A pride of lions is made up of related female lions and their young, as well as a few males. Males leave the pride when they are about three years old.

MEDIUM-SIZED CATS
Medium-sized cats, including lynxes and pumas, are able to kill large prey, such as deer and antelope, but unlike the biggest cats, they can survive on smaller food items like rats and mice when large prey are scarce. Pumas, for instance, kill elk up to seven times their own weight as well as small ground squirrels. Cheetahs specialize in snagging running gazelles. This accounts for their "uncatlike" greyhound build and their retractable claws that are always unsheathed and ready to provide traction during high-speed chases.

SMALL CATS
The remaining cats, all under roughly 40 pounds (18 kg), hunt small prey—birds, mice, fish and even small snakes and large insects. These are the same prey your cat brings home so you can admire its skill. But unlike lions, which might go days between each huge meal, small cats must hunt much more persistently. Female ocelots, for instance, might spend up to 18 hours every day hunting food for themselves and their young.

DESERT-DWELLER
Part of the Domestic Cat lineage, the sand cat lives in the desert and preys on the same foods as the domestic cat, including small birds and mice.

THE BABY OF THEM ALL
At around 2.5 lb (1 kg) the black-footed cats are the world's smallest species of cat.

FAST AND FURIOUS
Cheetahs are the only cat to rely on speed rather than stealth. Their legs are adapted for running at great speeds, not for climbing.

energy from a steady diet of small prey. In Asian forests, tigers hunt deer, wild pigs and wild cattle that range from 150-pound (68 kg) axis deer to 2,000-pound (900 kg) gaur. On the African plains, lions kill antelope, wildebeest and buffalo in a similar size range. But the habitats in which lions and tigers live have resulted in very different lifestyles.

Tigers are typically solitary cats, living and hunting alone except for mothers and young cubs. In the cover of forest, a tiger can secretly kill and settle down to its meal in peace. Lions, on the other hand, hunt in the open and other lions quickly close in to see what they can grab from a kill. It takes a group to defend a kill, so lions have evolved a social lifestyle, living in groups called prides. The core of that social life is a group of related females—mothers, sisters, daughters, aunts and their young. While these female groups are permanent, groups of males come and go, joining a pride when they can oust the resident males, and staying until another male group ousts them. Curiously, feral domestic cats often adopt a social lifestyle similar to that of lions.

THE DOMESTICATION OF THE CAT

The ancient Egyptians are known to have adopted cats for domestic use. Taken on sea voyages because of their ability to kill rodents, cats gradually spread throughout the world.

How and at what period various species of wild cat became domesticated is hard to establish. While it is possible that cats dwelt in farming villages in the Middle East as long as 10,000 years ago, conclusive evidence, from ancient Egypt, is dated to about 2000 BC.

As the way of life changed from nomadic to agrarian, people had to ensure that they had sufficient food supplies to last from one harvest to the next. Although the grain was kept in storehouses, it could never be fully protected against mice and rats that were able to sneak through cracks.

In their search for food, wild cats frequently wandered into settlements, hunting down and feeding on the increasingly abundant mice and rats. The farmers quickly realized how useful the cats were in killing the vermin and protecting their grain supplies and, unlike dogs, which had long been domesticated, cats were especially useful because they were predatory at night when the mice and rats were feeding. Rather than chase the cats away, the farmers set about encouraging them to stay, first by feeding them and

THE SACRED CAT

By 1500 BC, the cat was considered a sacred animal in Egypt and was represented in countless works of art, including this bronze cat dated *c.*30 BC.

EGYPTIAN CHARM
Bast, Bastet or Pasht, as represented in this gold charm c.1040 BC, was the Egyptian goddess of love and fertility. She had the head of a cat and the body of a woman.

rights to owning a cat, while the Pharaoh, who was of divine status, could. The cats were still permitted to live in the homes of the people, but had to be brought to the storehouses at night to catch vermin before being allowed to return home in the morning.

Cats' status as demigods ensured that they were worshipped and pampered, and they were soon being immortalized in paintings and sculptures. Severe punishments were inflicted if a cat was harmed, and if one was killed, the punishment was death.

When a cat died, the Egyptians would enter a period of mourning, demonstrating their grief by such means as shaving off their eyebrows. The cat would be mummified and, in an elaborate

eventually by petting them. And, with an endless supply of food at hand and protection from enemies, the cats became disinclined to wander in the wild.

DEMIGOD STATUS

It is thought that in about 1500 BC, the Pharaoh of Egypt had a supply of grain of such magnitude that he needed more cats to protect it. As people were unwilling to part with their cats, it is believed that the Pharaoh proclaimed all cats demigods. This meant that a normal mortal had no

TOMB PAINTINGS
To understand the esteem in which cats were held, scholars study paintings such as this fragment of papyrus (c.1295–1069 BC). Here, cats are shown herding a flock of geese. Such items are common finds in ancient Egyptian tombs.

MUMMIFICATION
In accordance with their high status, dead cats were embalmed and placed in coffins before being buried in cat cemeteries, many of which were located near the temple of Bast, or Bastet, in the ancient city of Bubastis (near modern-day Zagazig). This mummy is dated c.332–30 BC.

PERUVIAN NOSEPIECE
Such was their popularity that cats were represented in innumerable artworks. This group of cats embellishes a gold nose ornament from Peru.

ceremony, was buried in a wooden or bronze casket in a cat cemetery. Archeologists have found more than 300,000 cat mummies at one cemetery in Beni-Hassan, Egypt.

SEA VOYAGES

Sailors also needed to protect their grain and food supplies from mice and rats and so began to take cats with them on sea voyages. It is thought that Greek and Phoenician traders first took the domestic cat to the Middle East and present-day Italy in about 1000 BC.

Domestic cats were gradually introduced into Asia and Europe, eventually reaching England. They continued to be taken on ships and, as exploration and trade grew in importance in the 1600s, the cat spread throughout the New World.

EUROPE

Although initially loved in Europe, with the Romans considering the cat a symbol of liberty and the guardian of the home, the cat experienced a fall from grace that was to last for over two centuries. In England, by the fourteenth century, the cat had come to symbolize evil and was closely

GIRL'S BEST FRIEND
French Impressionist Pierre Auguste Renoir (1841–1919) depicts the cat as a loving companion in his work *Girl with a Cat*.

STORIES IN PICTURES
This Roman vase (c.450–400 BC) depicts two ladies, a cat and a pigeon.

ASIA

Cats are highly respected creatures throughout Asia. In some parts of Asia, they were used in temples to protect manuscripts from being eaten away by rats and mice. They also helped prevent rats and mice from attacking the silkworm cocoons. The silk trade was of vital economic importance to China and Japan. In fact it was so important to China that the talents of the silkworm were kept secret for 3,000 years and anyone who revealed the secret faced a penalty of death.

In Siam (present-day Thailand), cats could be owned only by royalty—the Siamese was once known as the royal cat of Siam.

HARD AT WORK
Two magic cats (below) go about their task of protecting the silkworms in this work by an unknown Chinese artist. If rats gnawed the cocoons, the precious silk would be ruined.

associated with witchcraft and the Devil. Hundreds of thousands of cats were burned to death, with the Church not only condoning the slaughter but actually championing and encouraging it.

As cat populations dwindled, the rat population grew. The culmination of this was the bubonic plague, or Black Death, which began in 1334 and quickly spread throughout Europe. This fatal disease is transmitted to people by rat fleas. The importance of cats in the control of rodents was once again recognized, and their popularity in the home gained momentum. By the late 1600s cat flaps were being installed in many households in France, enabling the family pet to come and go as it pleased.

PERENNIAL FAVORITES
An earthenware jug from Southwark, England c.1670. Potters, painters, quilters and tapestry makers have all been charmed by the cat, seeing it as a source of inspiration for their work.

VARIATIONS IN APPEARANCE

While cat breeds vary only slightly in their morphology, the variety of head and ear shapes, eye shapes and colors, and hair types, colors and patterns is almost endless.

THE SPICE OF LIFE
The American Shorthair has a moderate-sized body with a modified round head. Its eyes are almond shaped and it has a dense, thick coat that comes in a large variety of colors and patterns.

Cats' bodies range from the short, thick and cobby body of the Persian, Manx and Exotic Shorthair to the long, lean and tubular body of the Siamese and Oriental Shorthair. In between there are the more moderate body types that strike a balance between the cobbiness of the Persian and the svelteness of the Siamese. They include such breeds as the Burmese, American Shorthair and Havana Brown.

HEADS
The shape of cats' heads can be divided into three basic types—wedge shaped (or triangular), round and rectangular. Siamese and Oriental Shorthairs are just two examples of breeds with wedge-shaped heads. Breeds such as the Abyssinian and Turkish Angora have a modified wedge, which is still triangular in shape but instead of sharp angles, it is gently curved or rounded. A round head is found in breeds such as the Persian,

Siamese—wedge-shaped head

British Shorthair—round head

Maine Coon—rectangular head

Scottish Fold—round eyes

Somali—almond eyes

Siamese—slanted eyes

Japanese Bobtail

Siamese

Ragdoll

Exotic Shorthair and British Shorthair. A modified round head (one that is not so round) would include such breeds as the Burmese, Manx and American Shorthair. A rectangular head is broad across the eyes and tapers down to a slightly narrower muzzle, giving the overall look of a rectangle. Both the Maine Coon and Havana Brown fall into this category.

EYES
Although all eyes are round, some cats' eyes appear to have a different shape because of the eye opening, or aperture. There are only three basic shapes—round, almond (or oval) and slanted. Cats with round eyes include the Burmese, Exotic Shorthair and Persian. Cats with almond-shaped eyes include the Abyssinian and American Shorthair. Cats with slanted eyes include the Siamese and Oriental Shorthair.

If you are planning to breed or show your pedigreed cat, eye color must conform to the coat color in all breeds,

except those permitted to have any eye color, such as the Manx, Scottish Fold and the Rexes, to mention only a few. Most other breeds must have the correct eye color for their color class (see *A Guide to Breeds* starting on p. 116).

TAILS
Cat tails come in many different sizes and shapes, from the short thick tail of the Persian to the tailless Manx. While the Japanese Bobtail has a tail that resembles a pompom and extends out from the body no further than a couple of inches (5 cm), the Cornish Rex, Siamese and Oriental have long, slender and almost whip-like tails. Other long tails, but not as slender, can be found in the Turkish Angora, Maine Coon, Ragdoll and Russian Blue. Other breeds, such as the Burmese, Exotic, American Shorthair and British Shorthair, have medium-length tails.

Exotic

red Selkirk Rex, longhair

EARS

The size, shape and placement of a cat's ears differ widely from breed to breed. They range from small to large, wide to narrow at the base, set high to low on the head, with pointed to rounded tips. There are the small, forward-folded ears of the Scottish Fold and the folded-back ears of the American Curl. Other small ears include those of the Persian and Exotic Shorthair, which are set far apart, almost to the sides of the head. Medium-sized ears set moderately far apart are found on the Burmese and British Shorthair, while tall, almost donkey-like ears that are strikingly large, set close together and bolt upright belong to the Cornish Rex.

The ears of the Devon Rex are very wide at the base, and are set so far apart and low down on the sides of the head that the cat looks quite elfin. The distinctive triangular ears of the Siamese and Oriental Shorthair are set to almost flare out and continue the lines of the triangular head.

HAIR

As a result of cross-breeding, there is now a huge variety of hair lengths and types. Lengths range from the Sphynx, with almost no hair, to the full, thick and flowing coat of the Persian. Between these two extremes are the short-haired breeds, such as the Cornish Rex, Burmese, Russian Blue and Siamese, and the medium-haired breeds, such as the Abyssinian, Balinese and Somali. Some cats have double coats, such as the Manx, Somali and Russian Blue, while others should be fine, silky and close lying, such as the Burmese, Siamese, Oriental and Bombay.

There are hundreds of color combinations with some hair colors having a different texture. For example, white hair is normally soft and silky, blue hair is cottony and more dense, and black hair is usually harsher and with a thicker texture, as are the ticked and tabby hairs.

The hair on some cats is actually one of their more distinctive features, such as the Selkirk Rex, which looks like a woolly sheep; the Devon Rex, with its loose, soft waves; and the Cornish Rex, with its short, tight waves. Other coats, such as those of the Russian Blue and Exotic Shorthair, are so dense and plush that running your fingers through them is a sensory pleasure.

Russian Blue

tortie and white Sphynx

COLORS   PATTERNS   SHADED COLORS

BASIC COLORS
Blue-eyed white
Copper-eyed white
Odd-eyed white
Black (ebony)
Cream
Blue
Red
Chocolate
Lilac (lavender)

OTHER COLORS
Golden
Cameo
Brown
Silver
Fawn
Cinnamon

COLORPOINTS
Lilac point
Chocolate point
Blue point
Seal point
Red point
Tortie point
Lynx point
Torbie point

TABBY COLORS
Cream
Brown
Blue
Red
Chocolate
Lilac
Silver
Cameo
Golden

TABBY PATTERNS
Classic
Mackerel
Spotted
Ticked (agouti)

TORTOISESHELL
Red and black (basic)
Blue cream
Lilac cream
Chocolate cream

PARTICOLOR
Calico (red, black and white)
Chocolate calico (red, chocolate and white)
Blue calico (red, blue and white)
Lilac calico (red, lilac and white)
Bicolor (white with any basic color or white with tabby color)
Van (white with a smaller area than the bicolor of any basic color, mainly on head, tail and legs)
Calico Van (white with a small area of any two basic colors, mainly on head, tail and legs)

TORBIE
Tabby colors
Tortoiseshell colors
Tabby with white
Torbie with white
(can also come in colorpoints and white)

Shaded coats are:
   Chinchilla
   Shaded
   Smoke

Chinchilla, Shaded and Smoke tipping can be added to:
   Basic solid colors
   Bicolor
   Golden
   Calico
   Cameo
   Tabby
   Torbie
   Tortoiseshell
   Van

solid hair

smoke hair

shaded hair

chinchilla hair

AGAINST THE GRAIN
Each of a cat's hairs can be a solid color or be ticked or shaded to various degrees with black or a color, ranging from the lightly tipped chinchilla to smoke tipping. The coat of a smoke may look like a solid color, but when you run your hand over it against the grain, a magnificent pale undercoat is revealed.

ebony Oriental

air • American Wirehair • Balinese • Bengal • Birman • Bombay •

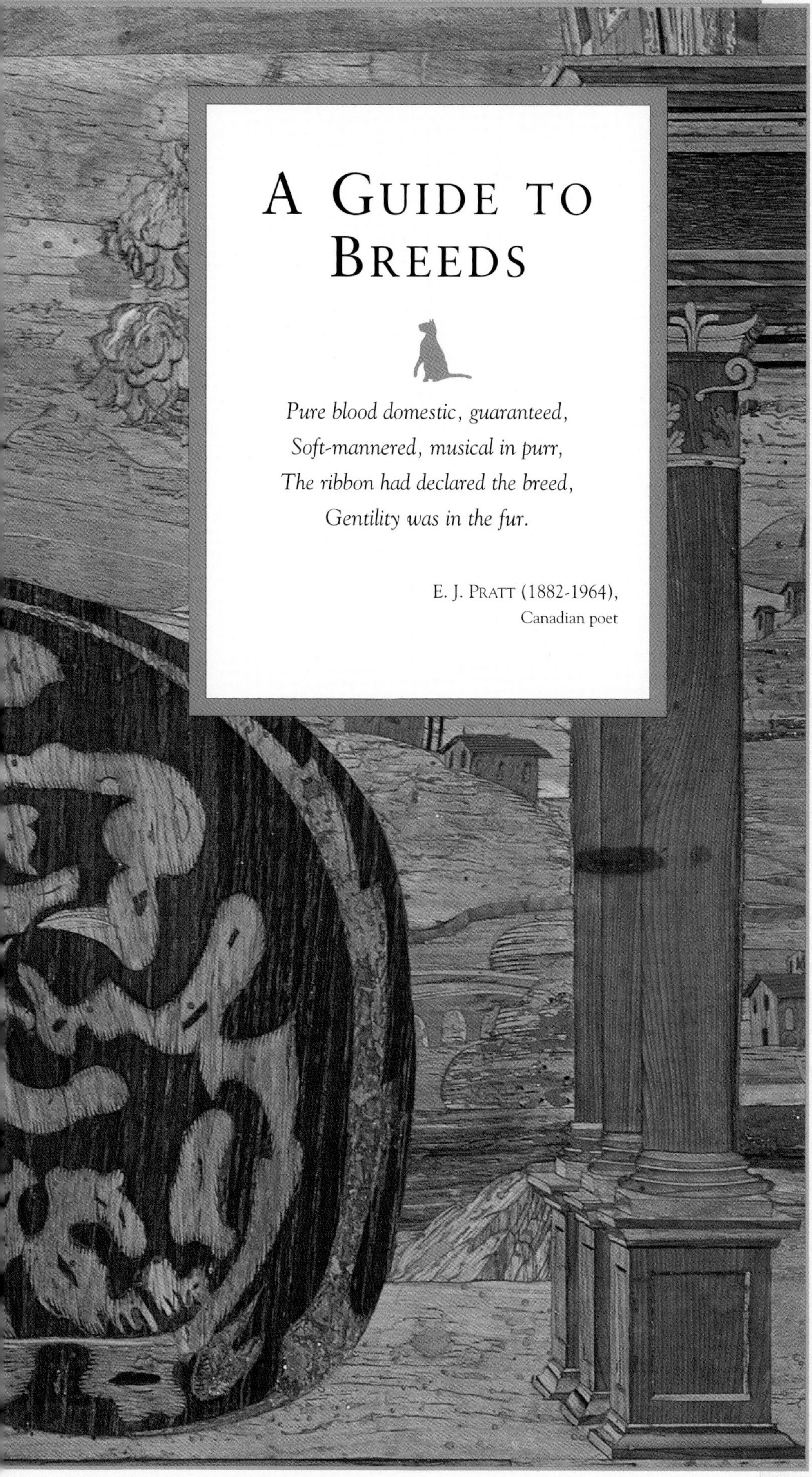

A Guide to Breeds

Pure blood domestic, guaranteed,
Soft-mannered, musical in purr,
The ribbon had declared the breed,
Gentility was in the fur.

E. J. Pratt (1882-1964),
Canadian poet

British Shorthair • Burmese • Chartreux • Cornish Rex • Devon Rex • Egyptian Mau • Exotic • Havana Brown • Japanese Bobtail •

Korat • Maine Coon • Manx • Munchkin • Norwegian Forest C

How to Use the Guide

This guide to 38 breeds is the perfect place to start the search for your ideal cat. With all the relevant information at your fingertips, you're well on the way to finding a cat that's just right for you.

NAME OF BREED
Breeds are presented in alphabetical order for easy cross-referencing.

INTRODUCTION
A brief introduction to the breed and its characteristics.

HISTORY
A general history of the breed, giving its origin, any cross-breeding and other interesting information, including when it was accepted as a breed and recognized for championship status.

DESCRIPTION
The form of the breed is outlined, including the ideal shape of the body, head, eyes, ears and tail. The length and texture of the hair is also given, along with grooming requirements.

Ocicat

A relatively recent arrival on the show scene, the spectacular spotted Ocicat has the beauty and athleticism of the wild cat with the disposition of the domestic cat. This appealing animal is a perfect choice for a family.

PET FACTS

- Daily hand grooming
- Warm climate only
- Short, tight, smooth
- Easily trained and very affectionate

DID YOU KNOW?
Although the Ocicat was named for its resemblance to the ocelot, it is not related to it and has no wild blood at all.

kittens

HISTORY
The first Ocicat appeared unexpectedly in a litter from a crossing of a ruddy Abyssinian with a seal point Siamese. This kitten eventually matured to a large, ivory cat with bright golden spots and copper eyes. The Michigan breeder, Virginia Daly, named the cat Tonga, but Daly's daughter called Tonga an Ocicat because of his resemblance to an ocelot. After Tonga's birth in 1964, other breeders followed the same crossing to develop more of the intriguing Ocicats. Later the American Shorthair was added to the mix to broaden the genetic base. The Ocicat was accepted for championship competition in 1986.

cinnamon

DESCRIPTION
The medium to large Ocicat has a rather long, well-muscled body that is solid and hard. It should look athletic and lithe, not bulky or coarse. The head is a modified wedge and there is a gentle rise, in profile, from the bridge of the nose to the brow. The broad muzzle finishes with a suggestion of squareness and the chin is strong. The neck is gracefully arched. The large eyes are almond shaped and are angled slightly up toward the ears. The moderately large ears are wide set and continue the outward lines of the face; they are neither flared nor upright. The medium-long legs are well muscled, with oval feet. The tail is fairly long, slim and tapered, and tipped at the end with a dark color.

172

GROOMING
Preferred grooming manner and frequency.

CLIMATE
Preferred climatic conditions.

HAIR/COAT CHARACTERISTICS
Length and texture in summary.

TEMPERAMENT
Brief summary of temperament.

PET FACTS

Daily hand grooming

Warm climate

Short, tight, smooth

Easily trained and very affectionate

DID YOU KNOW?
Although the Ocicat was named for its resemblance to the ocelot, it is not related to it and has no wild blood at all.

DID YOU KNOW?
An interesting piece of information about the breed.

OCICAT

The coat is short, smooth and satiny in texture with a lustrous shine. It is tight and close lying and there should be no suggestion of woolliness. All the hairs are ticked in a banded pattern, except the tip of the tail, which is solid. The forehead is marked with an intricate tabby "M" extending up over the head and breaking into small spots on the lower neck and shoulders. Rows of round spots run along the spine from the shoulder blades to the tail. Spots sprinkle the shoulders and hind-quarters, and extend down the legs. The belly is also well spotted and the eyes are ringed with mascara markings. Very little grooming is necessary, beyond regular hand grooming and an occasional brushing.

VARIETIES
The Ocicat comes with spots in an array of eye-catching colors: tawny (brown-spotted tabby), chocolate, cinnamon, blue, lavender, fawn, silver, chocolate silver, cinnamon silver, blue silver, lavender silver and fawn silver. The ground colors range from white to ivory to bronze. All eye colors are accepted, except blue, and there is no correlation between the eye color and coat color.

TEMPERAMENT
Because of its Siamese, Abyssinian and American Shorthair ancestors, it exhibits some of the qualities of all three. It becomes very attached to the people in its family but is not demanding. It does well in a household with other cats or dogs and is usually extroverted and friendly with strangers, bright and easily trained. Being very sociable, it doesn't like to be left alone for long periods.

chocolate

blue

VARIETIES
Details regarding the various color and pattern combinations available are given according to show standards. Where there is mention of a "preferred" or "accepted" characteristic, this refers to what is most desirable or allowable for show purposes.

TEMPERAMENT
This section discusses the breed's general traits and habits to help you decide whether or not this particular cat will fit in with your family and other pets, and with your lifestyle.

IMAGES
A number of varieties of the breed are illustrated in different poses so the reader can easily identify the cat. The animals photographed are not necessarily of professional breeder quality.

173

Abyssinian

With its sleek, ticked coat, the Abyssinian strongly resembles a small wild cat. It is highly intelligent and extremely active, and although it is not a lap cat, it is loyal and affectionate and makes a wonderful companion.

ruddy

red

HISTORY

One of the world's oldest known breeds, the Abyssinian looks like the paintings and sculptures of ancient Egyptian cats and still retains the jungle look of *Felis lybica*, the African wildcat ancestor of all domestic cats. Although its origin is uncertain, the early specimens of the breed were taken to Britain by soldiers returning from the Abyssinian War in 1868. They were first recognized as a separate breed in Britain in 1882 and although they were first exhibited in the U.S. in 1909 they were not recognized as a separate breed there until 1986. Several top-quality Abyssinians that arrived in North America from England in the late 1930s form the foundation of today's American breeding programs.

DESCRIPTION

The ideal Abyssinian has a slim body of medium size and length. Adult animals are lithe, hard and muscular with all physical elements of the cat in proportion. The head is a modified wedge and the brow, cheek and profile show a gentle contour with a slight nose break; the ears are large and alert. The almond-shaped eyes are large, brilliant and expressive and may be gold, green or hazel with a dark rim. Abyssinians move gracefully on their fine-boned legs and give the impression that they are standing on tiptoe. The tail is of medium length, broad at the base and tapered, without kinks.

The lustrous coat is beautiful to feel—soft, silky and fine in texture but also dense and resilient. The hair of this colorful cat should be long enough to accommodate dark, distinct bands of ticking.

VARIETIES

In the U.S., the Abyssinian comes in ruddy, red, blue and fawn. All colors must have at least two bands, preferably three, of ticking on each hair. Faint broken necklace marks around the throat are faults, and a solid unbroken necklace is cause for disqualification on the show bench.

The ruddy Abyssinian is a burnt sienna, ticked with black or dark brown. The undercoat and inside of the forelegs and belly are a paler orange-brown and

fawn

PET FACTS

- Daily hand grooming
- Moderate climate
- Medium–short, dense
- Active and inquisitive

DID YOU KNOW?
The earliest Abyssinian taken to Britain was called Zula. Its owner was the wife of Captain Barrett-Lennard and its picture appeared in a book published in 1874. Zula bears little resemblance to today's Abyssinians.

should be free of tabby markings. The ears and tail are tipped with black or dark brown, the paw pads are dark brown and the nose leather is tile red.

The red, or sorrel, Abyssinian is a warm, rich red, distinctly ticked with reddish brown. Deeper shades of red are preferred with an undercoat of apricot. The ears and tail are tipped with reddish brown and the paw pads and nose leather are rosy pink.

The blue Abyssinian is a soft, warm blue, ticked with various shades of slate blue. The undercoat and inside of the forelegs and belly are a warm cream to beige. The tail tip and outer tip of each hair is dark steel blue. The paw pads are mauve and the nose leather is dark pink.

The fawn Abyssinian is a warm beige ticked with dusky fawn, the outer tips of the hairs being darkest. The undercoat and inside of the forelegs and belly should be an unmarked pale fawn. The ears and tail are tipped with dusky fawn or lilac, the paw pads are mauve and the nose leather is pink.

In addition to these four colors, The

blue

International Cat Association (TICA) also recognizes the Abyssinian in the following colors—sorrel silver, blue silver and fawn silver.

The sorrel silver Abyssinian is medium white to light sorrel, ticked with chocolate brown.

The blue silver Abyssinian is silvery blue-gray, ticked with a deeper blue. The underside color is white to pale cream.

The fawn silver Abyssinian has a silvery, pinkish buff body, ticked with a deeper shade of pinkish buff. The underside is white to pale oatmeal.

TEMPERAMENT

Highly intelligent, the gentle Abyssinian has a well-balanced temperament, is eager, active and shows a lively interest in its surroundings. It is a great companion cat, delighting in your company and always curious to know what you are doing. However, don't expect it to settle down as a lap cat as it usually has far too much unexpended energy. Confident, well-mannered and responsive, it loves to play and will quickly devise spontaneous little games to hold your attention. It has a small and bell-like voice.

American Curl

The backward-tipped ears of the American Curl make it unmistakable. Curious and companionable, these attractive cats adapt easily to almost any home situation and tolerate the presence of other animals remarkably well.

brown classic tabby and white longhair

HISTORY

Although its history is very brief, this breed has already gathered a growing band of admirers. The first American Curl was a black longhair female kitten of unknown parentage that appeared on the doorstep of Joe and Grace Ruga's home in Lakewood, California, in 1981. Captivated by her unusual ears, they kept her, calling her Shulamith, meaning "black but comely." All American Curls must trace their pedigree to Shulamith, the foundation female.

In December 1981, Shulamith delivered a litter of four kittens, two with the same curly ears as their mother. A geneticist was consulted to study this phenomenon and he confirmed that the unusual ear was a genetic trait and that the gene was dominant, with no deformities attached to it.

Selective breeding and presentation in shows of American Curls began in 1983, and they are now accepted in all associations in the U.S. They enjoy good health and come in all colors and patterns, with both long and short hair. The International Cat Association accepted the breed for registration in 1985 and granted it championship status in 1986. The breed is, as yet, not recognized for showing in Britain.

DESCRIPTION

The American Curl's body is medium sized, elongated in shape with moderate strength and tone. The head is a modified wedge, longer than it is wide, with a straight nose and a muzzle that is neither pointed nor square. It is an elegant and alert animal with a sweet and friendly expression. The eyes are walnut shaped, moderately large and may be any color, with no particular relationship to the coat color, except that blue eyes are required in colorpoint classes. Legs are of

silver ticked shorthair

medium boning and the feet are medium sized and rounded. The tail is wide at the base, tapered and equal in length to the body; the longhaired American Curl has a beautiful plumed tail.

The outstanding feature of the American Curl is its remarkable curled ears. At birth, the ears are straight but they begin to curl back during the first ten days of life. The degree of curl is not finally established until the kittens are about four months old. Care should be taken when handling the ears— never force the ear into an unnatural position or you may break the cartilage.

The degree of curl to the ears is of paramount importance in show specimens. There should be a minimum of 90° arc and a maximum of 180° of curl. The cartilage should be firm from the base of the ear to at least a third of its height. The ears are wide at the base and open, curving back in a smooth arc when viewed from front and rear. The tips must be rounded and flexible.

Since the curl of the ear is the major identifying feature of the American Curl, the standard calls for disqualification of any cat if its ears curl to such an extreme that they touch the back of

red classic tabby longhair

the ear or head, or if the ears are straight or severely mismatched in the degree of curl.

The coats of both longhair and shorthair types are soft and silky with minimal undercoat and no ruff. Grooming is easy because the hair does not mat—regular combing and an occasional bath will keep these intriguing cats looking good.

VARIETIES
American Curls come in all colors and patterns. Choose from a glistening snow-white with azure blue eyes, or a silver tabby with emerald-green eyes. Since they have such a wide gene pool (Curls can be mated to any other breed that matches their physical conformation), you can find an American Curl with any color coat, including colorpointed, and any eye

color that you wish. Because it is their unique curled ears that set them apart, any color, eye color or coat length is acceptable for showing.

TEMPERAMENT
Curious and friendly, the impish American Curl enjoys human company and remains playful and kitten-like throughout its adult life. These cats are very affectionate, even-tempered, lively and intelligent, and quickly make friends with new human acquaintances.

brown spotted shorthair

American Shorthair

A handsome and gentle companion, the hardy American Shorthair has earned its place on the hearth of American homes since pioneering days. Long-lived and problem-free, it gets along well with other family members, including dogs.

silver classic tabby kittens

HISTORY

The ancestors of today's American Shorthairs arrived in North America with early European pioneers. They made themselves useful aboard ships by catching the rats that ate the food supplies and that spread disease among humans. Once ashore, these hard-working cats bred freely and eventually established themselves as North America's own shorthaired cat. Through the years they have been called both Domestic Shorthair and American Shorthair, but since the 1950s the latter term has prevailed. The first shorthair placed in the official U.S. register in 1901 was an imported male British Shorthair orange tabby. There is a large genetic component from the British Shorthair breed in the American Shorthair, however, these cats are now rather larger than their British cousin, with less rounded faces and longer legs and tails.

blue classic tabby

DESCRIPTION

The medium to large American Shorthair is a true working cat. Its body should be strong, athletic and well proportioned. These cats are not fully grown until three or four years of age, with males usually being significantly larger than females. The head is large with a full-cheeked face, slightly longer than it is wide. The medium-length nose has a gentle concave rise in profile. The nose leather is in harmony with the coat color. The strong-jawed muzzle is squared, and mature males have definite jowls. The bright, clear eyes are large and wide with the upper lid shaped like half an almond and the lower lid a fully rounded curve. They should slant slightly up at the outside end and the

The medium-length legs are sturdy and well muscled, and the paws are full and rounded with the pad color in harmony with the coat color. The medium-length tail tapers to a blunt tip and should have no kinks.

Short, thick, even and coarse in texture, the coat is dense enough to protect the cat from cold, moisture and superficial skin injuries. It thickens up considerably in winter, but is not as plush as that of the British Shorthair. Grooming entails no more than regular combing to remove dead hair and a wipe over with a damp chamois to make the coat shine.

color must conform to the coat color. The medium-sized ears are set fairly well apart and the expression is both trusting and friendly.

PET FACTS

- Regular combing
- Can tolerate cold weather
- Short, thick, coarse
- Friendly, intelligent and independent

DID YOU KNOW?
An American Shorthair brown tabby was sold for $2,500 at the Second Annual Cat Show at Madison Square Garden, New York, in 1896.

shaded silver

blue cream

brown patched tabby

VARIETIES
There are more than 100 colors and patterns to choose from in the American Shorthair and everyone seems to have a favorite. This is just a tiny sampling.

Silver tabby: white ground color with dense black tabby markings arranged in a specific pattern. The classic pattern is most distinctive and consists of one or more unbroken necklaces on the chest, three wide circular lines forming a bullseye on either side of the body, ring marks on the tail, bracelet marks on the legs and a shape like a butterfly with outspread wings on the shoulders. It is sometimes referred to as the "jewelry" pattern. With its emerald eyes, the silver tabby is truly a show-stopper.

White: a pure glistening white fur. The nose leather and paw pads are pink and the eyes are brilliant copper, vivid blue or odd-eyed (one copper and one blue).

Black smoke: the undercoat is white with the end of each hair deeply tipped with black (until it moves, the cat looks solid black). The points and mask are black with only a narrow band of white on each hair near the skin. The nose leather and paw pads are black and the eyes are copper.

Blue tabby: the ground color, including lips and chin, is pale bluish ivory; the markings are deep blue. The nose leather is deep rose, the paw pads are rose and the eyes are brilliant copper.

Blue-cream: blue with clearly defined patches of solid cream well broken up all over the body, legs and tail. The nose leather and paw pads are blue and/or pink and the eyes are brilliant copper.

Shaded silver: white under-coat with black tipping shading down from the face, flanks and tail, from dark on the spine to white on the chin and the underparts of the body and tail; the legs should be the same shade as the face (the cat should look darker than a chinchilla). The rims of the eyes, lips and nose should be outlined in black. The nose leather is brick red, the paw pads are black and the eyes are blue or blue-green.

white

Brown tabby: the ground color is coppery brown with dense black markings in any of the tabby patterns. The lips, chin and rings around the eyes are paler and the backs of the legs are black from the paw to the heel. The nose leather is brick red, the paw pads are black or brown and the eyes are brilliant copper.

Van bicolor: the body is mainly white with unbrindled patches of any one color, largely confined to the head. The nose leather and paw pads are pink or harmonize with the color of the patches and the eyes are copper.

Blue: light blue (lighter shades preferred) and an even tone from the nose to the tip of the tail. A sound darker shade is more acceptable than a slightly patterned lighter shade. The nose leather and paw pads are blue and the eyes are copper.

chocolate chinchilla

cream mackerel tabby

black smoke

TEMPERAMENT

No matter what the color and pattern combination, the American Shorthair displays the same even temperament and friendliness. It is a perfect companion, both indoors or to accompany you on outdoor treks. Its robust, muscular build and protective coat lend themselves to walks in the rain or in cold temperatures. The American Shorthair is an excellent hunter with quiet ways, combined with a gentle, playful nature, which makes it an ideal choice for families.

127

American Wirehair

An extraordinary coarse, wiry coat distinguishes this still quite rare cat from all other breeds. The attention-grabbing American Wirehair makes an intelligent and most affectionate pet, with a vast range of pattern and color possibilities.

HISTORY

Wirehaired cats have been observed in natural colonies from time to time in the past, but have died out with natural breeding. The first known American Wirehair was one of a litter of six barn cats born in 1966 in Verona, New York. He was named Adam. He had sparse, wiry hair, and every hair was crimped, coiled and springy, even the whiskers. Every American Wirehair now traces its parentage back to Adam.

The breed was accepted for championship competition by the Cat Fanciers' Association of the U.S. in 1978. It is largely unknown outside North America.

DESCRIPTION

The Wirehair is a well-boned, medium to large cat with well-developed muscles, very similar in type to the American Shorthair. The rounded head has prominent cheekbones and a well-developed muzzle and chin. In profile, the nose shows a gentle concave curve and the nose leather should harmonize with the coat color. The large, round eyes are bright and clear and may be any color, not necessarily corresponding to coat color. The medium-sized ears are set wide apart on the head. Sturdy legs, in proportion to the body, finish in compact paws with pad color in keeping with the coat. The tapered tail is medium length with a rounded tip.

Wirehair kittens are born with tightly curled coats. In the mature animal, the hard, frizzy, medium-length coat still feels springy, tight and resilient. Individual hairs, including the hairs inside the ears, are crimped, hooked or bent. The overall appearance of wiriness and the coarseness and resilience of the coat is more important than the crimping of each hair. The density of the wired coat leads to ringlet formation rather than clean waves. Curly whiskers are also desirable. Grooming is minimal. An occasional brushing with a soft brush to remove dead hair is all that is required.

VARIETIES

The Wirehair comes in any and all coat colors and patterns, except colorpoint, solid chocolate or solid lavender because these are

brown mackerel tabby

128

evidence of hybridization with a Siamese or Himalayan. The only requirement for show purposes is the wiriness of the coat. Unfortunately, in this breed as in others calling for certain characteristics, many of the kittens do not have the prized feature.

Anyone breeding Wirehairs must be prepared to find good homes for such straight-coated cats, which are not eligible for showing.

TEMPERAMENT

Since the American Wirehair is closely related to the American Shorthair, you can expect it to have the same affable nature. The Wirehair is friendly and plays in a gentle manner, getting along famously with children and with other pets, including dogs. It is quiet and reserved with lovable ways.

PET FACTS
Occasional light brushing
Can tolerate cool weather
Medium, crimped, hard
Friendly to people and other animals

DID YOU KNOW?

If you stroke the coat of an American Wirehair in one direction, it feels as soft as silk. But stroke it in the opposite direction, and you will think you are touching a mass of steel wool.

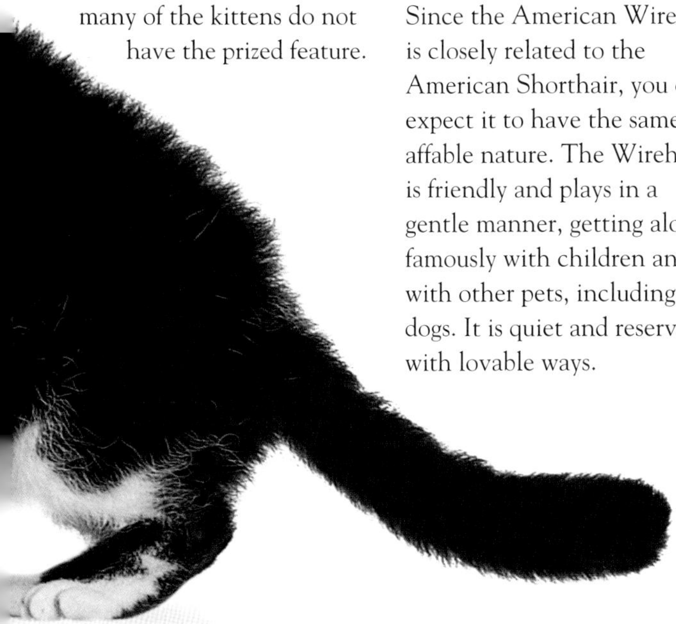

black and white bicolor

calico van

Balinese

With its gently swaying tail, the Balinese is the epitome of natural grace. It looks regal and aristocratic, like a Siamese in a spectacular pale ermine coat. Intelligence shines in its brilliant sapphire eyes and its inquisitive nature makes it a wonderful pet.

seal lynx point

DESCRIPTION

A light-bodied cat, the Balinese is exactly like a Siamese except for its coat. It has a long tubular body and is sleek, svelte and well muscled. It has fine bones with narrow shoulders and hips, which continue the body's sleek lines. The abdomen should be tight with no evidence of obesity or emaciation. The head is a long tapering wedge. The nose is long and straight with no break and the nose leather should harmonize with the coat color. The muzzle is fine and wedge-shaped, the chin and jaw must be firm, neither receding nor excessively massive, and the neck should be long and slender. The deep, vivid blue, almond-shaped eyes slant up from the nose. The ears are strikingly large, pointed, wide at the base and continue the lines of the head's wedge.

The long, slim legs end in dainty, oval paws with the pad color harmonizing with the coat color. The tail is long and thin, tapering to a fine point, with its

blue point

HISTORY

During the 1930s and 1940s, many Siamese breeders tried to produce a longhaired Siamese by crossing them with Angoras. Most of the offspring, however, were shorthaired and the breeders gave up. It later became apparent that many of the shorthaired offspring were carrying a recessive long-haired gene and it wasn't long before two such cats were mated and produced a Siamese with a longer coat. An early champion of the breed proposed the romantic name Balinese for her beloved longhaired Siamese. Her choice was adopted and these cats have been known as Balinese ever since. The breed gained championship status in the U.S. in 1963.

red lynx point

covering of hair spreading out like a plume.

The coat is medium length rather than long, but may be longer on the underbelly, around the neck and on the tail. The texture is fine and silky, with no downy undercoat. For this reason, the coat does not mat and grooming is simple—regular combing and brushing is enough to maintain its beautiful appearance. While the original Balinese had long flowing coats, repeated breeding to Siamese to achieve the desired type has lessened the length of the coat. Indeed, you might very well see a Balinese today with nothing more than a few wisps on its belly and a slightly fuller tail to indicate that it is not a Siamese.

VARIETIES
The Balinese is a colorpoint cat and comes in seal point, blue point, lilac point, chocolate point, red point, tortie point and lynx point. The red points, tortie points and lynx points are called "Javanese" by the Cat Fanciers' Association, but Balinese by all others.

TEMPERAMENT
The Balinese is a slightly toned down version of its Siamese cousin. It is intelligent, active and inquisitive, but does not have a loud voice. Some of the longhaired ancestors are perhaps responsible for these cats being somewhat less vocal and having softer voices. They dislike being left on their own and can be mischievous if they are bored and lonely. The answer to this could be to have two cats.

chocolate point

lilac point

Bengal

With its sinewy body and spotted coat, the Bengal looks like a small leopard—its jungle colors combined in spotted or marbled patterns, conjure visions of the wild. Careful consideration should be given before acquiring a Bengal as it could behave threateningly.

seal lynx spotted tabby

HISTORY

The present-day Bengal was created in the late 1970s by a Californian breeder who wanted to reproduce the spotted pattern, colors and facial qualities of the Asian Leopard Cat. She inherited eight females, the products of crosses between Asian Leopard Cats and domestic shorthairs, from a researcher at the University of California at Davis. She then added two males to this breeding group: a feral, orange domestic shorthair with deep brown rosettes from a zoo in Delhi, India; and a brown-spotted tabby domestic shorthair from a shelter in Los Angeles.

The only association that accepts the Bengal for championship showing in the U.S. is The International Cat Association (TICA). None of the other associations will allow it to enter, because their bylaws prohibit the showing of any cats with wild blood, no matter how far back in the pedigree it may be. The Bengal now holds championship status with TICA.

DESCRIPTION

With its large, sleek body, the Bengal looks basically wild. It will wade through water with no hesitation. It is strong boned and very muscular, particularly the male. The head is a broad modified wedge, longer than it is wide, with rounded contours, much like its wild ancestors, but slightly smaller in proportion to its body. The neck is thick-set, muscular and large in proportion to the head. The nose is large and wide with slightly puffed, brick red nose leather outlined in black. The muzzle is full and broad with large, prominent whisker pads. The large eyes are almond shaped. They are blue-green in the seal sepia tabby, seal mink tabby and brown tabby, and blue in the seal lynx point. The ears are short, like its wild ancestors.

The medium-length legs have large bones and the feet are large and round

brown marble

with black paw pads. The medium-length tail is thick, with a rounded black tip.

The thick, luxurious, medium-length coat is soft and needs only an occasional combing to keep it looking good.

black spotted leopard kittens

VARIETIES

The Bengal comes in both spotted and marbled patterns and in brown tabby, seal lynx point, seal sepia tabby and seal mink tabby. Ground colors may be ivory, cream, yellow, buff, light or dark tan, golden, orange and mahogany; patterns may be black, dark brown, brown, tan, chocolate or bitter chocolate and cinnamon. The cheeks, chin and throat are white.

TEMPERAMENT

The main controversy surrounding the Bengal hinges on its temperament. Offspring of original Leopard Cat crosses and even third- and fourth-generation offspring from the Wild Leopard Cat can revert to the wild and attack without warning. Domestic cats may also be upset by the pungent odor of their urine. Unfortunately, to retain the unique wild-looking spotted pattern, breeders are forced to go back to original crosses and first- and second-generation Bengals, thereby perpetuating the wild behavior. Breed enthusiasts recommend that anyone wanting a Bengal as a pet should ascertain that it is at least five generations removed from the wild cat ancestor. For show purposes, the Bengal must be unchallenging and any sign of threatening behavior will result in disqualification.

black spotted leopard

brown spotted tabby

Birman

A gorgeous cat with sapphire eyes, the Birman is known as the Sacred Cat of Burma. Its long, sumptuous coat and beautiful coloring would be enough to win admirers, but it also has intelligence, good health and a gentle temperament.

lynx point kitten

HISTORY

The origin of the Birman is lost in legend, but it was once considered sacred, a companion cat of the Kittah priests in Burma. Earlier this century, two Birman cats were clandestinely shipped from Burma to France. The male did not survive the long voyage, but the female, Sita, did and, happily, was pregnant. From this small foundation, the Birman was established in the Western world. The French cat registry recognized the Birman as a separate breed in 1925, but Britain did not follow suit until 1966. It gained recognition in the U.S. in 1967.

DESCRIPTION

Ideally, the Birman is long, large and stocky. It has a strong, broad, rounded head with a Roman nose of medium length. The face has a sweet expression, with full cheeks, a somewhat rounded muzzle and a strong chin. The medium-sized ears are set far apart on the head and have rounded tips. The blue eyes are quite round and deeper shades are preferred.

The Birman has heavy-boned legs of medium length. Its paws are large and round, and all four are white; these are the Birman's distinguishing feature. The white gloves on the front feet, preferably

seal point

seal point kitten

mat if it is brushed regularly to remove dead hair. The pale coat sometimes looks as if it has been dusted with gold. The "points"—mask, ears, legs and tail—are darker, like those of the Siamese and Himalayan.

VARIETIES

The Birman comes in seal point, chocolate point, blue point and lilac point. Recently, some Birmans have appeared in the colors of red point, tortie point and lynx point, but these are not as yet recognized anywhere in the world for championship showing.

symmetrical, usually end in an even line across the paw at, or between, the second or third joints. Those on the back paws should cover all the toes and extend up the back of the hock (the first joint). These leg markings are called "laces." Ideally, the front gloves match, the back gloves match, and the two laces match. Faultlessly gloved cats are rare and the Birman is judged in all of its parts as well as the gloves. The paw pads are pink or pink spotted with the point color. The tail is bushy and of medium length.

The longhaired, silky hair is not as thick as that of the Persian and doesn't

PET FACTS	
🪮	Daily combing and brushing
☁	Can tolerate cool climate
🐈	Semi-long, silky
🐈	Gentle and quietly active

🐾 **DID YOU KNOW?**
By the end of World War II there were only two Birmans left in Europe. Cross-breeding was necessary to establish the breed once more.

TEMPERAMENT

The gentle Birman has a delightful personality and is active, playful and independent. It makes a good pet for children.

lilac point

blue point kitten

Bombay

Although it was named after the great Indian city because of its resemblance to that country's black leopard, the Bombay's similarity ends with the coat. This sleek and handsome cat has a gentle, loving nature.

kittens

HISTORY

Created in the late 1950s and early 1960s, the Bombay is the result of crosses between the Burmese and black American Shorthairs. Kentucky breeder Nikki Shuttleworth Horner, a keen fancier of the cross, was instrumental in having the new breed recognized and, after a great deal of lobbying, championship status was awarded to the Bombay in 1976. It is rare outside the U.S. and is still awaiting recognition in other countries, including Britain.

DESCRIPTION

A medium-sized cat, the Bombay is well balanced, muscular and surprisingly heavy for its size with the male being a little larger than the female. Its head is rounded with no sharp angles; the face is full with round eyes set far apart and a short, well-developed muzzle tapering slightly. In profile, there should be a visible nose break and the nose should not present a "pugged" or "snubbed" look. The medium-sized ears are set well apart and have rounded tips. Although the round, wide-set eyes may range in color from gold to a deep, brilliant copper, deep-colored or copper eyes are considered superior.

The legs are medium length and in proportion to the body, and the feet are small and oval. The tail is medium length, straight and free of kinks. The nose leather and paw pads are black.

The coat should be very short, fine and close-lying, and should gleam like satin.

It is extremely easy to groom, needing only regular combing with a fine-toothed comb to remove dead hair and perhaps a wipe over with a silk cloth or damp chamois to give it the shine of patent leather. Because little hair is shed, these cats are especially suited to a totally indoor situation.

VARIETIES
The Bombay comes in only one color—black. Each hair must be jet black right down to the roots. The coat and color are considered so exceptional that in the standards of some American associations, half of the points (50) are allotted to the quality of the coat. In judging two Bombays of equal merit, the depth of eye color would probably be a deciding factor in choosing the winner.

TEMPERAMENT
Bombays are extremely smart and agile. They love plenty of company, enjoy games and fetch naturally, but may become depressed or naughty if deprived of company. Because they show great affection, they make most satisfying pets. The hybrid cross of the Burmese and black American Shorthair has made the Bombay hardier, healthier and less vocal than many other breeds.

British Shorthair

A robust and powerful cat with a rich, short, easy-care coat and a calm nature, the British Shorthair is a favorite in Britain, where it originated, and throughout the world. Its genes have contributed good qualities to many other breeds.

HISTORY

Perhaps the oldest of the English breeds and one of the least altered, the British Shorthair traces its ancestry from the domestic cat of Rome, which became established in Britain during the time of the Roman Empire. This breed was first prized for its physical strength and hunting ability, but soon became equally valued for its gentle nature, endurance and loyalty. It is still a robust and healthy breed with none of the problems that some of the greatly modified breeds encounter. Because the original color was blue, the British Shorthair was at one time known as the British Blue. When other colors, such as cream and then blue cream appeared, the name was simply changed to British Shorthair.

Although it was one of the first breeds to be shown in Britain late last century, it remained comparatively rare in the U.S. until about 1964, when it was recognized for championship competition there. A similar European breed, derived from Chartreux and British Short-hairs, is called the European Shorthair, but it is judged to the British Shorthair standard. There are two very distinct head types in the European Shorthair breed, according to whether Chartreux or British Shorthair predominates in the pedigree, and this makes judging difficult.

DESCRIPTION

The British Shorthair is a medium to large cat with a compact, well-developed body and a full, broad chest. Its broad, round, massive head is set on a short, thick neck. The face and underlying

PET FACTS	
🪮	Weekly combing
☁	Can tolerate cooler weather
🐈	Short, thick, resilient
🐈	Playful and companionable, but rather reserved

🐾 **DID YOU KNOW?**

The word "tabby" comes from the name of the old quarter of Baghdad, al Attabiya. Silk fabric patterned in black and white and known as "tabbi" in the West was once made there.

blue

blue and white bicolor

red mackerel tabby

bone structure are also rounded, as is the forehead, which is slightly flat on top of the head and should not slope. The medium-sized nose is broad and straight with the nose leather in keeping with the coat color. The chin is firm and in line with the nose and upper lip, and the muzzle is well developed with a definite stop behind large, round whisker pads. The large, round eyes are level and wide set, and come in copper. The medium-sized ears are broad at the base, with rounded tips.

The strong legs are short, well proportioned and heavily boned, with large, firm, round paws and paw pads that harmonize with the coat color. The tail is medium and thick and tapers to a rounded tip.

The short, thick, single coat is dense and resilient. A weekly combing to remove dead hair is all that is needed to keep it looking good, although many owners have a repertoire of tricks to enhance the appearance for show purposes.

VARIETIES
The British Shorthair comes in all colors and patterns, except solid chocolate, solid lilac and colorpoint. The tabby pattern is commonly seen in all colors in the classic, mackerel, ticked or spotted tabby form. The classic tabby pattern is discussed in the American Shorthair entry (see p. 126). Mackerel tabbies have narrow penciling of a darker shade all over the body, with rings on the chest and tail and

blue spotted tabby

139

even bars on the legs. In the ticked tabby, each hair is ticked with bands of the shades of the ground and contrast colors, and the cat must have at least one distinct dark necklace. The spotted tabby has spots instead of stripes or pencil markings. The spots should not run together, except for a dorsal stripe running the length of the body and tail. The tail and legs are barred.

Some of the popular color and pattern combinations for the British Shorthair include:

Blue: light blue (lighter shades preferred) and an even tone from the nose to the tip

of the tail. The nose leather and paw pads are blue and the eyes are copper.

Blue cream: the two colors cover the entire body in softly mingled patches (a blaze is desirable down the nose and under the chin, and a solid color on the legs, face or feet is a fault). The nose leather and paw pads are blue or pink, or mixed blue and pink and the eyes are copper. The blue cream combination occurs only on females, and blue cream kittens may look like plain blues at first.

Blue and white bicolor: mainly white with a certain percentage of distinct, unbrindled

dilute calico

patches of blue distributed all over the body; a white blaze on the face is desirable. The nose leather and paw pads are blue or pink and the eyes are brilliant copper.

Red mackerel tabby: the ground color is rich red with the lips, chin and sides of feet darker; the mackerel pattern is a rich, vibrant, mahogany red. The forehead is marked

cream spotted tabby

brown spotted tabby

with a characteristic "M" or "frown lines." The nose leather is brick red, the paw pads are deep red and the eyes are copper.

Blue spotted tabby: the ground color, including lips and chin, is pale bluish ivory with fawn overtones; spotted tabby markings are deep blue and the forehead is marked with a characteristic "M" or "frown lines." The nose leather and paw pads are blue or pink and the eyes are copper.

Cream spotted tabby: the ground color, including lips and chin, is pale cream; the spotted tabby markings are darker cream, but not too dark; the forehead is marked with a characteristic "M" or "frown lines." The nose leather and paw pads are pink and the eyes are copper.

Brown spotted tabby: the ground color, including lips and chin, is rich coppery brown; the spotted tabby markings are dense black; the forehead is marked with a characteristic "M" or "frown lines." The hind legs are black from the paw to the heel. The nose leather is brick red, the paw pads are black and the eyes are copper.

Black: glossy jet black with each hair an even tone from the root to the tip (no white hairs). The nose leather and paw pads are black and the eyes are brilliant copper.

Tortoiseshell and white (calico): bold patches of black and red on a white body (the three colors should be in roughly equal amounts; a blaze is desirable down the nose and under the chin). The nose leather is black or red, the paw pads are blue or pink, or a combination of the

blue cream

two, and the eyes are brilliant copper. The tortoiseshell and white combination occurs only on females.

TEMPERAMENT
The British Shorthair has a calm, gentle nature and is a loyal pet. Although it can be aloof, it becomes devoted to its owners, and makes a wonderful, undemanding companion that fits in well with family life. The female is an excellent mother.

black

Burmese

A sleek and elegant shorthair, the Burmese is agile and graceful with a delightful personality, good looks and great charm. Easy to look after and playful and tolerant of children, this is, many say, the perfect cat.

blue

HISTORY

Although Burmese cats have been recorded in their country of origin for at least 500 years, the modern breed has been developed in the U.S. only since 1930. The foundation animals were an Oriental-type female called Wong Mau, imported from Burma, and a seal point Siamese. At that time, the Siamese very much resembled the traditional Burmese in head and body characteristics.

Probably no breed has endured quite as much controversy as the Burmese. The Cat Fanciers' Association (CFA) withdrew recognition of it in 1941 because there were too few cats with three generations of descendants that bred true to type, and the breed was not reinstated until 1956. Although the original Burmese was a sable brown color, the only known brown cat in the fancy at that time, breeders began to produce other colors, notably champagne, in the early 1960s. The new colors caused an uproar, and the CFA opted to call them Malayan rather than Burmese, to soothe the ruffled feathers of purists who bred only sable Burmese.

In the mid 1970s, a more serious controversy arose. A Burmese with facial features markedly different from the standard and from other

Burmese was exhibited. The nose was so much shorter and the muzzle so much broader that it looked more like a brown Exotic Shorthair. Predictably, some judges pounced on this exhibit, pronounced it of "extreme type," and awarded it points over other Burmese.

platinum

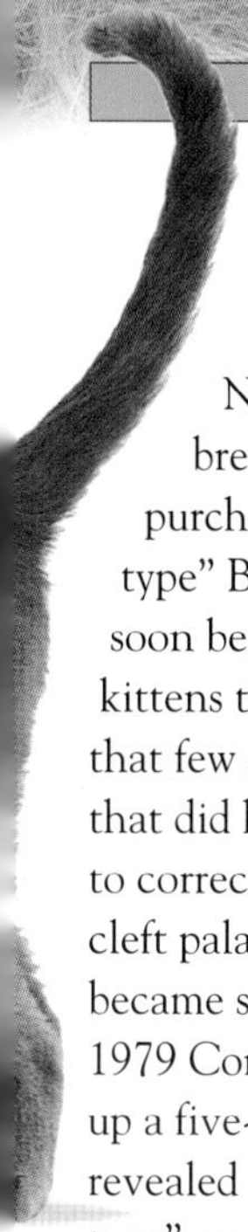

Naturally, many breeders rushed to purchase this "extreme type" Burmese, but defects soon began to appear in kittens to such an extent that few survived, and those that did had to have surgery to correct eye defects and cleft palates. The problem became so serious that in 1979 Cornell University set up a five-year study that revealed that the "extreme type" carried certain genetic flaws. The country remains divided with some preferring to retain the look and stamina of the traditional Burmese and others breeding to achieve the new appearance, which is now called "Contemporary."

British breeders imported their first Burmese from the U.S. in 1947 and the breed gained official recognition there in 1952. A whole spectrum of new colors and a lighter, more streamlined body,

PET FACTS

🪮 Weekly combing

☁ Needs warm climate

🐈 Short, fine, close-lying

🐈 Affectionate, amusing and companionable

🐾 **DID YOU KNOW?**
The Burmese is well known for its friendly, affectionate and trusting personality. Because of this characteristic, it should always be kept safely indoors.

sable

champagne

sable

structure and good muscle development. Its chest is rounded and the back is straight from the shoulders to the hips, with the hips as wide as the chest.

The head is a rounded, medium-sized wedge, with a full face and considerable breadth between the eyes. A broad, short, well-developed muzzle maintains the rounded contours of the head. In profile, there is a visible nose break and the chin is firmly rounded. The nose leather should harmonize with the coat color. The medium-length neck is well developed. The large, shining, expressive eyes are well rounded, set far apart and are a deep gold color. The medium-sized ears are set well apart and have rounded tips.

The legs are medium length and are well proportioned with small, round paws in the U.S. (oval paws in Britain) and paw pads in keeping with

the coat color. The tapered, medium-length tail should be straight with no kinks.

The gleaming coat is short, fine and satiny, and lies close to the body. Grooming entails only a weekly combing to remove dead hair and a wipe over with a damp chamois to enhance the natural shine.

VARIETIES

In the U.S., Burmese come in only four colors—sable, champagne, blue and platinum. In other countries, they also come in brown, blue, chocolate, lilac, red, cream, brown tortie, blue tortie, chocolate tortie and lilac tortie.

Sable (also known as brown) is the original and perhaps most

closer in type to the breed's Siamese ancestor has resulted from British breeding.

DESCRIPTION

The U.S. Burmese (pictured) is an altogether rounder and stockier animal than its counterparts in other countries. It has a compact, dense, medium-sized body with substantial bone

blue

striking color: the hair is rich, warm, sable brown, right down to the roots, shading to a lighter tone on the underparts. The nose leather and paw pads are brown and the eyes are brilliant yellow to gold.

Champagne (also known as chocolate): the hair is rich, warm, honey beige, with slightly darker shadings on the face and ears allowed. The nose leather is light warm brown, the paw pads are pinkish-tan and the eyes are brilliant, deep golden yellow.

Blue: the hair is rich blue, right down to the roots, shading to a lighter tone on the underparts. The nose leather and paw pads are slate gray with a pinkish tinge and the eyes are brilliant golden yellow. The ears, face and feet have a silvery shine.

Platinum (also known as lilac): the hair is pale, soft, silvery gray; ears and mask are slightly darker. The nose leather and paw pads are lavender-pink and the eyes are brilliant, deep golden yellow.

TEMPERAMENT

Burmese are extremely friendly to both strangers and family and communicate in sweet, soft voices. They crave attention and affection and will do anything to get it. They remain playful well into adulthood and dislike being left alone for long periods. If yours is a household where humans are absent throughout the day, perhaps you should consider keeping two cats for company. Females assume an active role in running the house, while males are more laid back and prefer to supervise from someone's lap.

sable

champagne

platinum

Chartreux

The sturdy French Chartreux is much admired for its hunting prowess and its dense, water-resistant fur. Its beautiful thick blue-gray coat has silver highlights and is set off by brilliant orange eyes.

PET FACTS

🪮 Daily hand grooming

🌥 Can tolerate cool weather

🐈 Medium-short, dense

🐈 Playful and gentle

🐾 **DID YOU KNOW?**
The Chartreux may have been named for a variety of Spanish wool of the early eighteenth century. The thick coat parts in places just like the fleece of a sheep.

HISTORY

Noted in French documents as early as the sixteenth century, the first Chartreux cats are thought to have been kept by Carthusian monks at the Grenoble monastery where the famous Chartreuse liqueur was made. The cats probably earned their keep by keeping rat and mice numbers down, and this home may be the origin of the breed's name, although there are many other possibilities. The Chartreux was first exhibited in Paris in 1931 by one of the Leger sisters, keen breeders from Brittany. Three of the first ten Chartreux to go to the U.S. in 1970 were obtained from the Legers' stock. In the U.S., the breed is classed as completely separate from the very similar blue British Shorthair, and received championship status in 1983.

DESCRIPTION

The chunky body of the Chartreux is medium length and solidly muscled, with broad shoulders and a deep chest, males being larger and heavier than females. Boning is strong and muscle mass is dense. The head is rounded and broad with powerful jaws, full cheeks and a softly contoured forehead. The nose is straight, medium length and width, with a slight stop at eye level. The muzzle is comparatively small, narrow and tapered, giving a sweet smiling expression. The neck is short and heavy set. The rounded eyes are moderately wide set and may be gold to copper, a clear, brilliant orange being the most favored color. The ears are small, set high on the head, with slightly rounded tips.

kittens

The legs are comparatively short and surprisingly fine-boned in comparison to the hefty body. The round feet are medium sized, which makes them appear almost dainty compared with the body mass. The tail is medium length, tapering to an oval tip. The double coat is soft and lush—especially thick on the adult male—and adds bulk to the appearance of both sexes. It is medium short and slightly woolly in texture (it should open like a sheepskin at the neck and flanks). It has a resilient undercoat and a long, water-resistant topcoat. Because brushing would damage the protective undercoat, it is best to use only a comb to groom your Chartreux about once a week. At other times, simply stroke the coat frequently, running your fingers through the fur and finish with a rub over with a damp chamois.

VARIETIES

The Chartreux comes only in blue, the soft blue-gray tones ranging from ash to slate. Each hair is tipped with silver, which gives the coat an iridescent shine. The nose leather is slate gray, the lips are blue, and the paw pads are rose-taupe.

TEMPERAMENT

Affectionate and gentle, the agile Chartreux makes a playful and delightful companion, but the tiny voice is a surprise in such a substantial cat. Its strength, intelligence and adaptability have enabled it to survive through centuries and these qualities should be preserved by breeders through careful selection.

Cornish Rex

*Playful and affectionate, the Cornish Rex is distinguished
by its unusual wavy coat like that of the Rex rabbit, from
which it derives its name. A born acrobat, lively and
intelligent, it makes a fascinating pet.*

PET FACTS

- Daily hand grooming
- Needs a warm climate
- Short, dense, soft
- Affectionate, playful and friendly

DID YOU KNOW?
Contrary to common belief, the Cornish Rex does shed hair, triggering allergies in susceptible people just as other cat hair does.

HISTORY

These highly unusual cats originated quite spontaneously, probably from a mutated gene, in Cornwall, England, as the name indicates. The first Cornish Rex appeared in a litter born in 1950 and the breed has fascinated geneticists ever since. Although several individuals sent to the U.S. in the late 1950s were developed independently of the Cornish strain, there is no noticeable difference between the two, and in fact, the Cornish strain is still predominant in the U.S. today. It was first accepted for championship competition in the U.S. in 1979 and is now accepted for competition worldwide.

DESCRIPTION

Lean and lithe bodied, the Cornish Rex has an arched back and a tucked-up stomach, something along the lines of a whippet. Its head is oval and comparatively small and its large ears are set high on the head. The high cheekbones and high-bridged Roman nose are unmistakable. The medium-sized oval eyes are very wide set, but their color is of secondary importance and need not conform to the shade of the coat. Whatever the eye color, it should be clear and intense.

The legs are very long and slender and the cat stands high on its feet, almost as if poised on tiptoe. The paws are dainty, slightly oval, and the paw pads should

red classic tabby

calico

black smoke

harmonize with the coat color. The tail is long, slender and flexible, with so little visible hair that it looks like a very fine whip.

The coat is most unusual. It is short, extremely soft, silky and completely free of guard hairs. Ideally, the fur lies close to the body, falling in washboard waves, like cut velvet or the fur of the Rex rabbit. The curls extend from the top of the head across the back, sides and hips, continuing to the tip of the tail. The fur on the underside of the chin and on the chest and abdomen is short and noticeably wavy. When the coat is stroked lightly, it feels incredibly soft, like the skin of a newborn chick. Grooming consists of regularly stroking the coat and an occasional wipe over with a silk cloth or a damp chamois to remove dead hair.

VARIETIES

The coat of the Cornish Rex may be any color or pattern, including color-pointed. Since it is the coat that sets this breed apart from others, it is of paramount importance in show judging and most standards allot almost 50 points of the tally to the coat alone.

TEMPERAMENT

Although it looks wary and sophisticated, the Cornish Rex is extremely affectionate and people oriented. It is an active cat that remains kitten-like well into maturity and it can be very inventive in its play. It likes to fetch and catch, even using its paws to toss small objects.

blue mackerel tabby

149

Devon Rex

The intriguing appearance and charming personality of the Devon Rex appeals to lovers of the unusual and exotic all around the world. Although a comparatively recent arrival on the cat scene, it has already won many staunch supporters.

black

chocolate
silver tabby

HISTORY
Like the Cornish Rex, the English Devon Rex originated from a single kitten in the early 1960s. This spontaneous mutation sported a curly coat, but strangely enough, although the coats of the two cats are so similar, the mutant gene is not the same. Many North American breeders obtained specimens in those early years and these have been crossed with the native American Shorthair in an attempt to provide an expanded and strong gene pool without losing the curly coat and pixie-like appearance. The Devon Rex was accepted for championship showing in 1982 and remains remarkably unchanged from its original conformation, head type, coat and disposition. It is now being bred worldwide.

DESCRIPTION
The muscular body is small to medium sized, with a good density of muscle. For such a small animal it is surprisingly heavy. The head is comparatively small and has a modified wedge shape, with a short muzzle and prominent cheek bones. The elfin face is full cheeked and the nose in profile has a strongly marked stop. The whisker pads are prominent. The strikingly large ears are very wide at the base and set very low on the sides of the head. The eartips are rounded and the ears are sometimes tufted. The oval eyes are large and wide set, sloping toward the outer

edge of the ears. Their color need not harmonize with the color of the coat.

The legs are very long and slim and the cat stands high on its small, oval feet, almost as if poised on tiptoe. The paw pads should harmonize with the coat color. The Devon Rex has a thicker tail than the Cornish Rex and it is not as whip-like. It looks even thicker than it is because the wave of the fur is looser and the tail comes to a blunt end rather than a pointed end.

Since the Devon Rex has less fur than most cats, it feels pleasantly warm on your lap. Although the Devon has some guard hair, the coat is not dense. The other hairs are downy soft and feel like incredibly smooth suede. The coat presents a rippling wave effect rather than the tightly waved look of the Cornish Rex. The wave is most apparent when the coat is smoothed with the hand. Grooming consists of wiping over with a silk cloth or a damp chamois to remove dead hair.

tortoiseshell

PET FACTS

Daily hand grooming

Needs warm climate

Short, soft, wavy

Lovable and friendly

DID YOU KNOW?
There is a danger of lameness with the Devon Rex and its breeding lines are being monitored closely around the world to eliminate this potential health hazard.

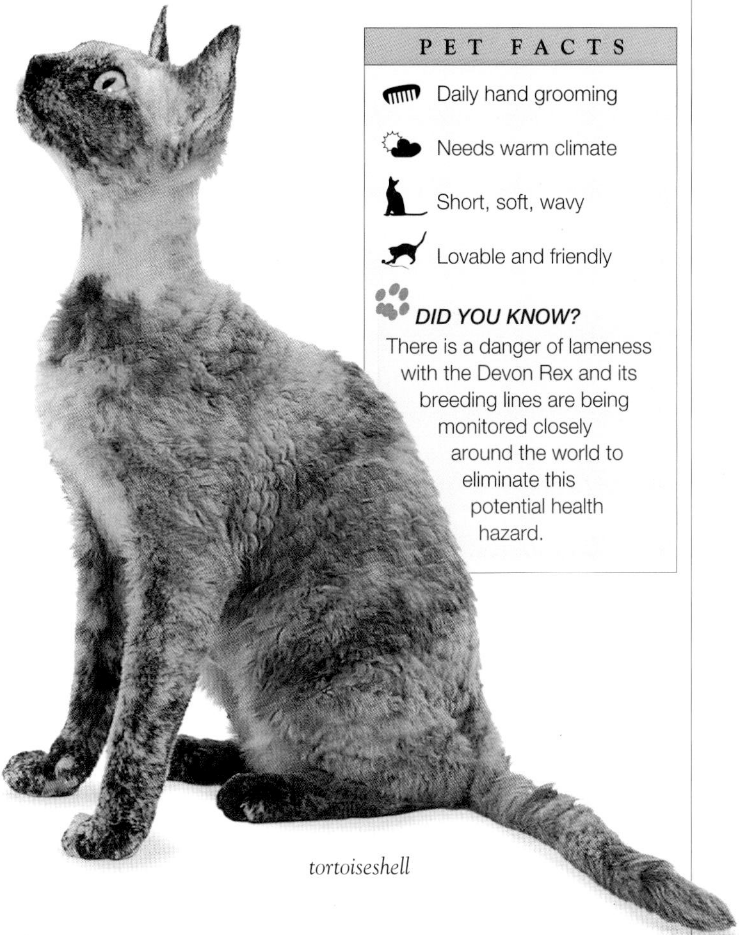

blue

VARIETIES
The Devon Rex may come in any combination of colors and patterns, including colorpointed. Its wavy, suede-like coat is one of its distinguishing features, along with its highly prized elfin or pixie look.

TEMPERAMENT
Although Devons love to play, they are also content to sit cozily in your lap. They are very affectionate and show it. They may mature more rapidly than some other breeds and the kittens are strong and mobile at birth.

Egyptian Mau

Elegance and grace are the hallmarks of the Egyptian Mau. Its beautifully marked coat and well-balanced temperament recommend it as a pet and, being the only natural breed of spotted cat, it also has rarity value.

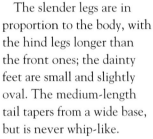

HISTORY

Thought to have originated naturally in Cairo, the Egyptian Mau (mau means cat) may be a descendant of the venerated cat of ancient Egypt. The American breed is based on just three animals imported from Egyptian stock in 1956 by an exiled Russian princess, Nathalie Troubetskoy. Until recently, Egyptian Maus in the U.S. and Canada all traced their ancestry to two of those original imports, but other animals have been brought in recently to broaden the available gene pool. The breed gained championship status in the U.S. in 1977.

DESCRIPTION

The graceful, muscular body of the Egyptian Mau is medium in length and size and is very strong.

The head is a slightly rounded wedge, medium in length. It is not full-cheeked and the profile shows a gentle contour from the bridge of the nose to the forehead. The ears should be medium to large and somewhat pointed, continuing the planes of the head. The rounded, almond-shaped eyes are large and alert, slanting slightly toward the ears. In adults, they are vivid green but the color develops as the cat matures.

bronze

The slender legs are in proportion to the body, with the hind legs longer than the front ones; the dainty feet are small and slightly oval. The medium-length tail tapers from a wide base, but is never whip-like.

The lustrous coat hair is medium length with a high shine. Little grooming is needed apart from a regular combing or rub over to remove dead hair.

VARIETIES

The Mau comes in four colors: silver, bronze, smoke and black. (The black Mau is not eligible for championship showing, but can be used in a breeding program.) In

152

silver and bronze, the hair is dense and must accommodate two or more bands of ticking. In the smoke color, the hair is fine and silky.

The silver ground color is a pale, clear silver, lighter on the underbody. Markings are black and contrast strongly with the ground color. The eyes are vivid green, the paw pads are black, and the nose leather is brick red.

The bronze ground color is a pale warm bronze, with a lighter beige on the underbody. Markings are dark brown and contrast strongly with the ground color. The eyes are a vivid green, the paw pads are dark brown and the nose leather is reddish brown.

PET FACTS

- Daily hand grooming
- Needs warm climate
- Medium, fine, silky
- Devoted and affectionate

DID YOU KNOW?
The Egyptian Mau particularly seems to enjoy being walked on a leash. A harness will give you more control.

The smoke ground color is a silvery white with jet black spots. The silvery white hairs have black tipping in the spotted areas and gray tipping in between, giving the coat a "sooty" look. Both feet and paw pads are black, and the nose leather, lips and vivid green eyes are outlined in black.

TEMPERAMENT
Very devoted, the Egyptian Mau is not an easy cat to transfer to a new owner. It is extremely intelligent and loyal and is thought to have a good memory. Active and playful, it indicates happiness by "talking" in a soft, melodious voice. The tail is also expressive and is wiggled at great speed to show delight.

silver

smoke

Exotic Shorthair

Blessed with a gorgeous coat that is much easier to look after than the Persian's, the Exotic Shorthair appeals to many people. Its temperament shows the best qualities of its varied ancestors, and it is also healthy and long-lived.

blue kitten

HISTORY

Before the Exotic was recognized for championship showing in 1967, many breeders of American Shorthairs (previously called Domestic Shorthairs) broke the rules by breeding them to Persians to improve the coat. The results of these matings did far better in the show ring than true Domestic Shorthairs with full pedigrees, but the practice led to falsification of pedigrees and surprises in litters when two "shorthairs" combined to produce longhaired kittens.

Finally, the Cat Fanciers' Association was persuaded in 1967 to establish a new breed called Exotic, to legitimize the combination of such diverse breeds as Abyssinians, Burmese, American Shorthairs and Persians. In recent years, however, the only breed that can legally be used to produce Exotics is Persian, and the breed now closely resembles the Persian in every way, except in the length of the coat.

DESCRIPTION

The Exotic is a heavily boned, well-balanced cat. Its body is stocky, low on the legs, broad and deep through the chest and equally massive across the shoulders and rump, with a well-rounded midsection and level back. Although it is a medium to large cat, the quality of characteristics is more of a determining consideration than size. The head is round and massive, with great breadth of skull. The face is round with round underlying bone structure, and is set on a short, thick neck. The nose is short, snub and broad, with a break between the eyes. The nose leather is in harmony with the coat color. The cheeks are full and the jaws broad and powerful. The brilliant eyes are large, round and full, set level and far apart.

blue

The ears are small with round tips, tilted forward and not unduly open at the base. They are set far apart and low on the head.

The legs are short, thick and strong and the forelegs are straight. The paws are large, round and firm, with pads to harmonize with the coat color.

blue cream kitten

The tail is short, bushy and in proportion to the body. It is normally carried low. The coat is dense, plush, soft and full of life, and has

PET FACTS

- Regular combing
- Can tolerate cool climate
- Medium, thick, plush
- A loyal companion, quiet and playful

DID YOU KNOW?
Even experienced cat breeders cannot tell which kittens in a litter of Exotics will be longhairs and which shorthairs.

brown classic tabby and white

black smoke

smoke tortie

cream point

a rich, thick undercoat. It stands well out from the body. Although very easy to groom, this needs to be done regularly, especially when the cat is shedding its winter coat, in order to avoid hairballs. Comb with a medium-toothed comb to remove dead hair and brush with a rubber brush.

VARIETIES
The Exotic Shorthair comes in all colors and patterns, including colorpoint. Their eye color must conform to their coat color in order to be shown. These are just a few from the vast selection of Exotics.

Blue: light blue (lighter shades preferred) and an even tone from the nose to the tip of the tail (a solid darker shade is more acceptable than a slightly patterned lighter shade). The nose leather and paw pads are blue and the eyes are brilliant copper.

Blue-cream: blue with clearly defined patches of solid cream well broken up all over the body, legs and tail. The nose leather and paw pads are blue and/or pink and the eyes are brilliant copper.

Smoke tortie: the ground color is white with the end of each hair deeply tipped with black and red in the clearly defined patches of the tortoiseshell pattern (until it moves, the cat looks like a tortoiseshell); a blaze on the face in red is desirable. The nose leather and paw pads are brick red and/or black and the eyes are brilliant copper.

Black smoke: the ground color is white with the end of each hair deeply tipped with black (until it moves, the cat looks solid black). The points and mask are black with only a narrow band of white on each hair near the skin. The nose leather and paw pads are black and the eyes are copper.

White: pure white fur with no shading or marking and no black hairs. The nose leather and paw pads are pink and the eyes are brilliant copper, blue or odd-eyed (one blue and one copper).

Chocolate: warm, medium to dark chocolate coat, even in color with no

chocolate

white

156

shading, markings or white hairs. The eye rims, nose leather and paw pads are chocolate and the eyes are brilliant copper.

Red tabby: the ground color is light red with rich, vibrant, mahogany red markings. The nose leather and paw pads are brick red to salmon pink and the eyes are brilliant copper.

Brown tabby and white: ground color, including lips and chin, is a rich tawny brown. Markings are black and the nose leather is brick red outlined with chocolate.

The paw pads are deep brown to black and the eyes are copper. Some associations require that the white portion comprises at least one third of the cat and includes an inverted "V" on the face. Others allow any proportion of brown tabby and white, with no preference given to the amount of white or lack thereof.

Tortie and white (calico): the coat is white with patches of red and black distributed in any proportion. The eyes are copper. The red and black may also be in a chinchilla, shaded, smoke or torbie pattern. Calicos also come in blue cream (called dilute calico by some), lilac cream or chocolate cream.

Colorpoint: the points and mask are darker than the ground color, but are in harmonious shades, and the nose leather and paw pads conform to the point color. The eyes are blue.

TEMPERAMENT
The Exotic has a lively, friendly, lovable nature and seldom makes a sound. It is a sweet and loyal companion, easy to live with and very affectionate.

red tabby

blue cream

Havana Brown

The picture of feline grace, the Havana Brown is a gentle creature, rather shy but very loving to its owner. Breeders worked long and hard to achieve this all-brown cat, the challenge being met in different ways in Britain and the U.S.

HISTORY

Although breeders had been trying since the 1890s to develop an all-brown cat, it wasn't until the early 1950s that crosses in Britain between a seal point Siamese and a black shorthaired cat with Siamese forebears produced the desired result. These cats, previously known as Chestnut Brown Foreigns, are the Havana Brown's foundation stock, but subsequent development in Britain and the U.S. took different paths. The first Chestnut Brown Foreigns were obtained by American breeders in the mid-1950s and the Havana Brown descended from those animals is now a much sturdier cat than the British Havana Brown. The breed was recognized for championship competition in Britain in 1958 and in the U.S. in 1959, under the name Havana Brown.

DESCRIPTION

These cats differ markedly in body type in the U.S., Britain and other countries. In the U.S., the Havana (pictured) has a moderate-sized, well-muscled body, striking a balance between the cobbiness of the Exotic Shorthair and the svelte length of the Siamese. The head is angular, longer than it is wide and in profile has a distinct nose break. The head of the English Havana is more like that of a Siamese. The head is longer than it is wide, narrowing to a rounded muzzle with a pronounced break on both sides behind the whisker pads. The somewhat narrow muzzle and whisker break are distinctive characteristics and must appear in all show specimens. When viewed in profile, there is an obvious stop at the eyes and the end of the muzzle appears almost square, making the profile quite unmistakable.

The oval eyes are set wide apart and there should be no sign of squinting. They are brilliant and expressive, in a vivid shade of mid-green.

PET FACTS

Twice weekly

Warm climate

Short to medium, smooth

Quiet and affectionate

DID YOU KNOW?
The Havana Brown possibly got its name because its coat is like the color of the Havana cigar.

The eye color develops slowly as the animal matures, and deeper shades are preferred. The ears are large with rounded tips, and they tilt forward. The legs are relatively long compared to the body, the legs of females being slim and dainty; the slenderness and length of leg will be less evident in a more powerfully muscled, mature male. The oval paws are compact and have either brown or rose-pink pads.

The short to medium-length coat is smooth, lustrous and needs only to be combed about twice a week with a fine-toothed comb. To bring up the gloss, simply rub a damp chamois over the coat.

VARIETIES

The Havana Brown comes in only one color, brown. It is best described as a rich and even shade of warm mahogany throughout—the color tends toward red rather than black. The coat should be free of tabby markings and the whiskers must also be brown. The nose leather is brown with a rosy flush.

TEMPERAMENT

From their mixed ancestry, these cats have picked up a grab-bag of traits to charm their owners. They are very curious and characteristically use their paws to investigate, touching and feeling anything that intrigues them. They are people oriented and crave human companionship.

Japanese Bobtail

Familiar to travelers as the cat with the raised paw in the china figurines sold in Japan as good luck symbols, the Japanese Bobtail is distinguished by its unusual short tail. This is preferably carried upright like a pompom.

Mi-ke longhair

red and white bicolor

HISTORY

Although the breed has existed in Japan for many centuries, it was unknown in the U.S. until 1968, when Elizabeth Freret imported the first three Japanese Bobtails from Japan. Breed standards were agreed on in the 1970s and the Bobtail was granted championship status in 1976.

At that time, it was known only as a shorthair, but a longhaired version was accepted for showing in 1993.

DESCRIPTION

The medium-sized body is long, lean and elegant, but not tubular like the Siamese. The head appears long and finely chiseled and forms a perfect equilateral triangle with gentle curving lines, high cheekbones and a noticeable whisker break. The nose is long with a gentle dip at or just below eye level. The large oval eyes are wide set and alert, but their color does not necessarily conform to the color of the coat. The ears are large, upright and have rounded tips. They are set wide apart so as to continue the lines of the triangular head.

The legs are long and slender with the deeply bent hind legs longer than the front. The hind legs are naturally bent when the cat is standing relaxed. The paws are oval with pads in a color that suits the coat. Each individual has its own variation of the unusual short tail, which is carried upright or close to the body curled like a pompom. The tail may be flexible or rigid, in harmony with the rest of the cat's body. It

black and white

VARIETIES

The Japanese Bobtail comes in all colors, except solid lilac, chocolate and color-pointed. The most popular color is called "Mi-ke" (mee-kay) which is white with red and black splotches, identical to what is called calico in the West. Another popular pattern is the bicolor. This is a white cat with one other color, either solid or patterned. If there are no more than two spots of color on the body, it is referred to as a van pattern. If there are more than two spots, it is called a bicolor.

must be clearly visible and comprise one or more curves, angles or kinks, or any combination of these.

The shorthair Japanese Bobtail has a medium-length coat that is soft and silky, but with no noticeable undercoat. The longhair has a soft, silky, medium to long coat that lies flat and follows the lines of the body. There is minimal shedding. A ruff is desirable, as are ear and toe tufts. Grooming entails only brushing with a soft bristle brush or a light combing.

blue and white,
odd-eyed

TEMPERAMENT

The Japanese Bobtail is active, intelligent and talkative; its voice is soft and it usually responds when spoken to. It is very adaptable, friendly and especially good with children. It loves human company, and has a lively and vivacious charm.

PET FACTS
Daily combing or brushing
Warm climate
Soft, silky
Intelligent, active and talkative

DID YOU KNOW?
China cats depicting this breed are often placed in shop windows in Japan. They have one paw raised in greeting and are called Maneki-neko, or "welcoming cats." They are thought to bring good luck.

Korat

With a winning combination of silver-blue fur tipped with silver, and large, luminous green eyes, who would argue at the Korat being called lucky? Certainly nobody in Thailand, where the breed has been esteemed for centuries.

HISTORY

Although found in all parts of Thailand, the Korat takes its name from one particular province. The earliest picture of this elegant cat, also known as the Si-Sawat, was found in a book of paintings in Bangkok's National Library. It is believed to have been painted during the Ayudhya Period of Siamese History (1350-1767).

At the time the first pair, Nara and Darra, arrived in the U.S. in 1959, the blue coat of the Korat was spotted with white and the tail was kinked, both traits considered unacceptable for showing. Through diligent breeding, these defects have now disappeared and the Korat was accepted for championship showing in the U.S. in 1966 and in Britain in 1975.

PET FACTS

🐾 Daily hand grooming

☁ Warm climate

🐈 Short, fine, glossy

🐈 Affectionate and playful

🐾 **DID YOU KNOW?**
In Thailand, a pair of blue Korats is often presented to a bride as a symbol of good fortune and to bring happiness to the marriage.

DESCRIPTION

The muscular, supple body of the Korat is semi-cobby, neither compact nor svelte, with males being heavier than females. The chest is broad and the back curved. The head is heart-shaped and very broad across the eyes, unlike any other breed. The eyebrow ridges form the upper curves of the heart and the sides of the face curve gently down to the chin to complete this attractive shape. The chin and jaw are strong and well-developed. In profile, the nose has a downward curve

open, and slightly slanted when closed or partly closed.

The slender legs should be in good proportion to the body, the front legs being shorter than the back. The paws are oval with pinkish lavender pads, and the medium-length tail has a rounded tip. Although some associations allow a kink in the tail (which can be felt but is not visible), others will disqualify the cat for this.

The short, single coat is glossy and fine, lying close to the body. The coat is inclined to part, or "break," over the spine as the cat moves. Grooming is easy, and regular combing will remove dead hair and minimize the possibility of hairballs forming. For a glossy shine, simply wipe over with a silk cloth or a damp chamois.

just above the leather, which is dark blue or lavender. The large ears have rounded tips and a wide flare at the base. They are set high on the head, giving an impression of alertness.

The prominent eyes are large and luminous green with extraordinary depth and brilliance. They may be yellow or amber with a green tinge around the pupil in young animals, but they change color as the cat matures. It may take up to four years before the green is fully developed. The eyes are well-rounded when fully

VARIETIES

The Korat comes only in blue. The coat is a solid silvery blue, each hair being tipped with silver, which should be sufficient to produce a halo effect. Where the coat is short, the silver shine is intensified. There should be no tabby markings.

TEMPERAMENT

These gentle cats love to romp, but dislike loud, sudden noises. They are calm and sweet-natured and enjoy human company, particularly children, and love to be stroked and petted. Their senses of sight, smell and hearing are thought to be unusually acute and they are excellent hunters.

Maine Coon

Large, powerfully built and impressive, the Maine Coon is healthy, active and good-natured. Whether it becomes a working farm cat, a treasured household companion or a show champion, it will always make its presence felt.

black

black and white

HISTORY

The Maine Coon, perhaps the earliest American breed, is probably descended from the first domestic cats to arrive on the North American continent. Early this century, these cats fell from favor with most breeders, who preferred to import longhairs with long pedigrees and without the white lockets, or markings on the neck, of the Maine Coons. Eventually, the Maine Coon disappeared from the show bench altogether, but its hardy genes were used to strengthen the Persian breed in the U.S., to the dismay of the same purists. It was not until the late 1950s that the Maine Coon gained championship status in its own right.

DESCRIPTION

One of the largest of all domestic cats, the Maine Coon has a muscular and broad-chested body that is much longer than the other longhaired breeds. Males are much larger and heavier than females. The large head is a broad, modified wedge of medium length with a squared off muzzle. The cheekbones are high. In profile, the medium-length nose is slightly concave. The wide-set eyes are large and expressive, slightly slanted toward the outer base of the ear. They may be green, gold or copper and do not

blue classic tabby

red tabby and cream tabby kittens

The lustrous, dense coat of the Maine Coon is shaggy and, with its slight but definite undercoat, heavy enough to protect the animal from a harsh climate. A frontal ruff is desirable. The hair is short on the face and shoulders, but longer on the stomach and hind legs, where it forms britches. The hair falls smoothly, following the lines of the body. Grooming consists of a light brushing every few days to remove dead hair. This should be enough to stop mats from forming.

PET FACTS

- Combing and brushing three times a week
- Can tolerate cold climate
- Long, heavy, shaggy
- Loving nature and talkative

DID YOU KNOW?
The Maine Coon loves to find small concealed places to sleep. This may be because they once earned their keep as ship cats.

necessarily conform to the coat color. Some white cats may have blue or odd-colored eyes. The ears are large, pointed, well-tufted and wide at the base. They are set moderately well apart and high on the head.

The medium-length legs are rounded, substantial and wide set, and the paws are large, round and well tufted, with pads that harmonize with the coat. The long tail is wide at the base with long, flowing hair and comes to a blunt end. No kinks are allowed in the tails of show cats.

VARIETIES
This breed comes in all colors and patterns except colorpointed, solid lilac and solid chocolate. There is often white around the mouth and chin of tabbies.

silver mackerel tabby and white

TEMPERAMENT
The gentle Maine Coon is known for its loving nature, calm disposition and intelligence, and especially for the soft little chirping noises it makes as it goes about its day. It is a delightful companion, loving and loyal and very patient with children. It is an excellent hunter and doesn't hesitate to go into water. It sometimes picks up food with its front paws.

Manx

The long-lived Manx is famous for having no tail, although many do have vestiges, and for being the symbol of the Isle of Man. It comes in almost every color and pattern imaginable and makes a charming family pet.

tortoiseshell and white longhair

brown patched mackerel tabby kitten

tailless trait in these cats, although legend supplies several far more fanciful explanations. Manx cats still abound on the island. Although the Manx was a popular and well-established breed in Britain before the birth of the cat fancy in the 1870s, it is no longer accepted for competition in shows sponsored there. The objection is that breeding this cat will perpetuate a lethal spine defect. It is accepted for showing in the U.S., however, and has been very popular there since about 1930.

HISTORY

The Manx cat originated on the Isle of Man, off the coast of England in the Irish Sea. The isolation of the island probably perpetuated the

DESCRIPTION

The Manx has the shortest body of any of the breeds. The chest is broad and the short back arches from the shoulders to the round rump. The head is round but slightly longer than it is wide, with prominent cheeks and a jowly appearance. In profile, there is a gentle dip in the nose. The nose leather should harmonize with the coat. The muzzle is slightly longer

red classic tabby

PET FACTS

🖌 Daily combing, especially longhairs

☁ Can tolerate cool climate

🐈 Thick, soft, plush

🐈 Intelligent and courageous

🐾 **DID YOU KNOW?**
Two completely tailless Manx cats must never be bred because the kittens are likely to have spinal deformities and die. One parent must have at least some vestiges of a tail.

red mackerel tabby longhair

than it is wide with a definite whisker break and large, round whisker pads. The neck is short and thick. The large eyes are round and full and set at a slight angle toward the nose. Eye color does not necessarily conform to coat color. The medium-sized ears are wide at the base, tapering gradually to a rounded tip and set far apart.

The hind legs are muscular and well boned and longer than the forelegs, which are short and set well apart, emphasizing the broad, deep chest. The rump sits considerably higher than the shoulders. The paws are round and the pad color should harmonize with the coat.

Show specimens have no tail, but these are hard to come by. Anyone interested in breeding Manx should be aware of the risks and high mortality rate of kittens. In fact, the last vertebra of the spine is missing, which results in a dip or hollow at the base of the spine where that bone

would normally be. Take care when handling such a cat—never pat the rump roughly as most Manx are sore and sensitive in that area. In spite of the spinal abnormality, the Manx is a speedy and powerful runner.

The double coat is short and thick in the Manx. In the longhaired version, also called the Cymric, the double coat is soft and silky, full and plush, falling smoothly over the body. It is best to groom both types often by gently brushing or combing with a medium-toothed comb. This will remove dead hair and prevent matting.

VARIETIES
The Manx comes in any color or pattern, including colorpointed, bicolor, solid and tabby.

TEMPERAMENT
The Manx is a playful cat and loves to perch on the highest possible point, even indoors. It will retrieve and bury toys as a dog does. It is generally good-natured and friendly.

black and white bicolor

Munchkin

For those who must have the very latest, no breed is more up to the minute than the Munchkin. Admirers of this short-legged charmer, as yet not widely recognized, are confident it has a big future.

black longhair

HISTORY

Cats with short legs are not new to science, although they have only recently been discovered by the cat fancy. In the 1944 veterinary record, Dr. H. E. Williams-Jones described four generations of cats with short limbs. The cats' movements were listed as being ferret-like. Unfortunately, these cats seemed to disappear during World War II, as did the bloodlines of many purebred cats. The Munchkin appeared spontaneously in Louisiana in the 1980s. From a pregnant black female found by Sandra Hochenedel in 1983, several colonies have now been established. These currently span multiple generations.

DESCRIPTION

At the present time, the Munchkin appears to come in every sort of body type, head type and coat length. The only thing these cats have in common is their extremely short legs. Since the gene pool is unlimited, there are no clear guidelines as to what type the Munchkin will ultimately resemble. Some Munchkin breeders are mating to Persians, others to Siamese and still others to Abyssinians.

At present, it is not possible to present a picture of the ultimate type, apart from its distinctively short legs.

In the studies that have been conducted so far, no skeletal changes have been associated with the short-legged gene and there is no evidence to suggest that these cats have any of the back problems of short-legged dogs, such as the Dachshund. This is undoubtedly because the cat spine differs markedly from that of the dog in its construction and flexibility, and spinal problems are rare

PET FACTS

- 🖌 Daily grooming
- ☁ Cool or warm climate depending on coat length
- 🐈 Variable length and type
- 🐈 Varies with ancestry

🐾 **DID YOU KNOW?**
The short legs of the Munchkin make it impossible for them to jump to escape predators.

tortie and white

seal point

odd-eyed white longhair

VARIETIES

At present, the Munchkin can have any type of head, body, coat or color. The only feature identifying it as a Munchkin is its short legs.

TEMPERAMENT

Since the Munchkin has so many different ancestors, its temperament will depend largely upon which cats are on its pedigree. As with any cat, the conditions under which it is raised and the amount of attention given during kittenhood are also factors in the temperament.

in cats. What the Munchkin does have in common with short-legged dogs is that the front legs are bowed. This does not seem to affect its climbing ability, but its jumping ability is limited by the shortness of the hind legs.

At present, Munchkins are accepted for championship competition in only one of the U.S. associations, The International Cat Association (TICA). The other associations have adopted a wait-and-see attitude for two reasons. One is to rule out the possibility of the shortened legs causing health problems in the cats in later life. The other is that because there is such wide disparity in type as a result of outcrosses to so many other breeds, it is difficult to set a type standard. Munchkin fanciers are confident that the eventual outcome will be a happy one for both them and the breed.

tortie and white longhair

Norwegian Forest Cat

A gorgeous, wild-looking animal, the Norwegian Forest Cat emerged from the forest and opted for domesticity and work on the farm some time during the past 4,000 years. Despite appearances, the coat is easy to care for.

blue and white

HISTORY

The Norwegian Forest Cat is an ancient natural breed that once lived in the woods of its native land. Although highly prized by Norwegian farmers for its superior hunting ability, no one else paid any attention to the cat until the 1930s. The breed almost became extinct during World War II, and owes its survival to Carl-Fredrik Nordane, a former president of the Norwegian Cat Association. In the early 1970s, he organized a breed club to champion and preserve the Forest Cat. The Feline International Federation of Europe (FIFE) granted it championship status in November 1977, and the first enchanting specimen arrived in the U.S. two years later. Because of its many similarities to the Maine Coon, it was not recognized there until 1987.

DESCRIPTION

The large body is medium length and solidly muscled with substantial bone structure and considerable girth. The chest is broad and the flanks have great depth. The triangular head has a wide, straight nose with no break in the line from brow ridge to tip. The nose leather should harmonize with the coat color. The chin is firm, in line with the front of the nose and gently rounded. The large, almond-shaped eyes are expressive, wide set and with the outer corner slightly higher than the inner. Eye color may be any shade of green, hazel or gold and white cats may have blue or odd-eyes. The ears are medium to large, rounded at the tip, upright and set far apart on the head. They do not flare out but follow the line from the side of the head.

The medium-length legs are heavily muscled with thickset lower legs. The paws are large and round and heavily tufted, with pad color in keeping with the coat. The magnificent tail is heavily furred, and remains so even in summer.

brown mackerel tabby and white

The water-resistant double coat is uneven in length with a dense, woolly undercoat and visible guard hairs in winter. The hair on the side of the face flows into a substantial ruff, framing the face like a full beard. The britches should be full. Daily combing is recommended when the winter coat is being shed but, unless it is destined for the show ring, the cat will take care of this itself. Surprisingly, the hair does not mat.

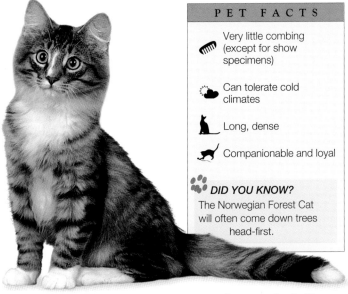

brown mackerel tabby and white kitten

PET FACTS

- Very little combing (except for show specimens)
- Can tolerate cold climates
- Long, dense
- Companionable and loyal

DID YOU KNOW?
The Norwegian Forest Cat will often come down trees head-first.

VARIETIES

The Norwegian Forest Cat comes only in longhair. Any color or pattern is acceptable, except colorpointed, solid lilac or chocolate. Popular colors include brown tabby, silver tabby and either of those with white. These colors originally helped the cat to blend into its woodland surroundings.

TEMPERAMENT

While the Norwegian Forest Cat is an excellent hunter and loves the outdoors, it also craves company. It loves to be handled and petted and returns this affection in full measure. As with other breeds, if a kitten is gently handled and exposed to children, cats and dogs from birth, the temperament will be more adaptable than that of one raised with limited human contact.

brown ticked tabby and white

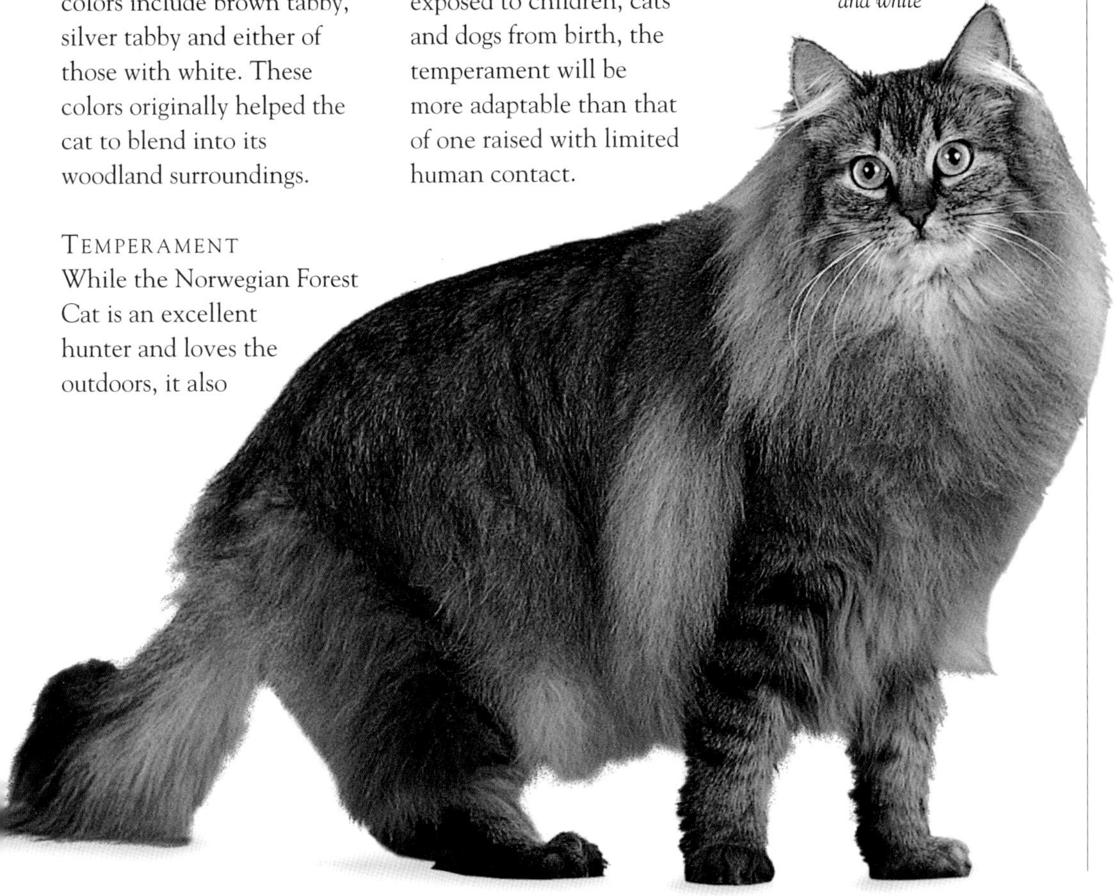

Ocicat

A relatively recent arrival on the show scene, the spectacular spotted Ocicat has the beauty and athleticism of the wild cat with the disposition of the domestic cat. This appealing animal is a perfect choice for a family.

kittens

PET FACTS

- Daily hand grooming
- Warm climate only
- Short, tight, smooth
- Easily trained and very affectionate

DID YOU KNOW?
Although the Ocicat was named for its resemblance to the ocelot, it is not related to it and has no wild blood at all.

HISTORY

The first Ocicat appeared unexpectedly in a litter from a crossing of a ruddy Abyssinian with a seal point Siamese. This kitten eventually matured to a large, ivory cat with bright golden spots and copper eyes. The Michigan breeder, Virginia Daly, named the cat Tonga, but Daly's daughter called Tonga an Ocicat because of his resemblance to an ocelot. After Tonga's birth in 1964, other breeders followed the same crossing to develop more of the intriguing Ocicats. Later the American Shorthair was added to the mix to broaden the genetic base. The Ocicat was accepted for championship competition in 1986.

cinnamon

DESCRIPTION

The medium to large Ocicat has a rather long, well-muscled body that is solid and hard. It should look athletic and lithe, not bulky or coarse. The head is a modified wedge and there is a gentle rise, in profile, from the bridge of the nose to the brow. The broad muzzle finishes with a suggestion of squareness and the chin is strong. The neck is gracefully arched. The large eyes are almond shaped and are angled slightly up toward the ears. The moderately large ears are wide set and continue the outward lines of the face; they are neither flared nor upright. The medium-long legs are well muscled, with oval feet. The tail is fairly long, slim and tapered, and tipped at the end with a dark color.

The coat is short, smooth and satiny in texture with a lustrous shine. It is tight and close lying and there should be no suggestion of woolliness. All the hairs are ticked in a banded pattern, except the tip of the tail, which is solid. The forehead is marked with an intricate tabby "M" extending up over the head and breaking into small spots on the lower neck and shoulders. Rows of round spots run along the spine from the shoulder blades to the tail. Spots sprinkle the shoulders and hind-quarters, and extend down the legs. The belly is also well spotted and the eyes are ringed with mascara markings. Very little grooming is necessary, beyond regular hand grooming and an occasional brushing.

VARIETIES

The Ocicat comes with spots in an array of eye-catching colors: tawny (brown-spotted tabby), chocolate, cinnamon, blue, lavender, fawn, silver, chocolate silver, cinnamon silver, blue silver, lavender silver and fawn silver. The ground colors range from white to ivory to bronze. All eye colors are accepted, except blue, and there is no correlation between the eye color and coat color.

TEMPERAMENT

Because of its Siamese, Abyssinian and American Shorthair ancestors, it exhibits some of the qualities of all three. It becomes very attached to the people in its family but is not demanding. It does well in a household with other cats or dogs and is usually extroverted and friendly with strangers, bright and easily trained. Being very sociable, it doesn't like to be left alone for long periods.

chocolate

blue

Oriental Shorthair

A comparatively recent development, Oriental Shorthairs already run the gamut of colors and patterns. Their sleek lines, intelligence and extroverted personalities come largely from the foundation of Siamese on which they were built.

lavender tabby

HISTORY

In the 1950s, a British cat fancier created a brown shorthair with green eyes and a Siamese body. Photographs of two such kittens appeared in the August 1954 issue of the British journal *Our Cats*. At first the chestnut brown kittens were called Havanas, according to some authorities, after the rabbit of the same color. Others say they were named after Havana tobacco. When the Governing Council of the Cat Fancy in Britain recognized these chestnut brown cats for championship competition in 1958, the name Chestnut Brown Foreign was chosen for the breed. In 1962, another British breeder and geneticist began working to produce a blue-eyed white cat of the same foreign type. These cats were not deaf, as some other blue-eyed cats are, and they were accorded championship status in Britain under the name Foreign White.

Peter and Vickie Markstein, two of the better-known Siamese breeders in the U.S., were so taken with the Foreign Whites and similar cats that in 1972, they decided to seek acceptance in the U.S. for all Foreign Shorthairs as one breed, to be called the Oriental Shorthair. The foundation stock for the

white longhair

174

Oriental Shorthair was the Siamese, from which comes the body type, plus American Shorthairs and Abyssinians, from which come the colors and patterns. The Oriental Shorthair was first accepted for championship competition in the U.S. in 1977 and all the other U.S. registries have since followed suit. In other countries, these cats are slightly smaller and are regarded as separate breeds called Orientals or Foreigns of various colors.

blue cream

DESCRIPTION

The body is like that of the Siamese, sleek, slender and refined in every respect. The medium-sized torso is graceful, long and svelte, combining fine bones and firm muscles. The shoulders and hips continue the tubular lines and the hips are never wider than the shoulders. The abdomen is tight and firm. The head is a long, tapering wedge, starting at the nose and flaring out in straight lines to the tips of the ears to form a triangle, with no break at the whiskers. The muzzle is fine and wedge-shaped. The tip of the chin lines up with the tip of the nose in the same vertical plane, neither receding nor excessively massive. The nose leather should harmonize with the coat color.

The almond-shaped eyes are medium size and slant upward from the nose, following the line of the head and ears. They should not be crossed and any hint of a crossed eye is grounds for disqualification on the show bench. The eyes are usually green, but white Orientals may have blue, green or odd eyes (one blue and one green). Ears are strikingly large and pointed, and open at the base. The legs are long and slim with dainty, small, oval paws. The paw pads should harmonize with the coat color. The long, thin tail tapers to a fine point and has no kinks.

The Oriental comes in both shorthair and longhair varieties. The short, fine coat of the Oriental Shorthair is glossy and lies close to body. An occasional combing to remove dead hair and a wipe over with a damp chamois to make the coat gleam are all that are needed by way of grooming. The medium-length coat of the Oriental Longhair is fine and silky

ebony ticked tabby

175

with no downy undercoat. It lies close to the body, except on the tail, which is long and feathery. More frequent combing is necessary to keep this type of coat in good condition.

VARIETIES
Both shorthair and longhair varieties come in many patterns and more than 300 colors. These include the normal solid colors, as well as chestnut, lavender, cinnamon and fawn, plus tabby patterns and spotted coats. With the addition of the silver gene, they also

blue ticked tabby longhair

come in smokes of all colors. It would not be possible to list all the color combinations, but a few of the most popular are:

White: pure white, with pale pink nose leather, dark pink paw pads and sapphire eyes.

Blue: even blue right to the root of each hair, lighter shades preferred in the U.S., with blue nose leather and paw pads and green eyes.

Ebony: pure jet black right to the root of each hair, with black nose leather, black or brown paw pads and emerald eyes.

Silver tabby: silver background with dense black markings, black or brick red nose leather rimmed with black, black paw pads and green eyes.

Lavender tabby (lilac in Britain): beige background with lavender gray markings, faded lavender or pink nose leather rimmed with lavender-gray, faded lavender paw pads and green eyes.

Red ticked tabby: bright apricot background with deep rich red markings, each hair is ticked with shades of apricot and red, pink or pink rimmed with red nose leather and blue paw pads. Green eyes are preferred in the U.S., green to copper in Britain. The face, legs and tail must show distinct tabby striping and there should be at least one distinct necklace.

Ebony ticked tabby (brown in Britain): warm coppery brown background with dense

ebony

black markings, each hair ticked with shades of brown and black, black nose leather or pink rimmed with black, brown or black paw pads, eyes may be rimmed with black and green is the preferred color. The face, legs and tail must show distinct tabby striping and there should be at least one distinct necklace.

Chestnut spotted: warm coppery brown background shading to creamy ivory on the undersides, with clearly defined markings of dark brown in a classic tabby pattern on the head and numerous round or oval spots on the back and legs, spots or broken rings on the tail, brick

red nose leather, black or dark brown paw pads and green eyes.

Smoke: pure white undercoat with the hair of the top coat tipped in one or more darker colors, the nose leather and paw pads are in keeping with the contrast color and green eyes. Any color is possible as the contrast color.

With such a tremendous range of possibilities, it is no wonder that these cats are becoming so popular worldwide. The only limit seems to be the imagination of the breeders.

red ticked tabby

white

TEMPERAMENT

Oriental cats are intelligent, gentle and love company. They dislike being left alone and can be mischievous if bored and lonely. They will do anything to get your attention and remain playful, high-spirited and affectionate well into maturity. The queens have large litters and are careful and loving mothers. The kittens don't change color as they mature as Siamese kittens do.

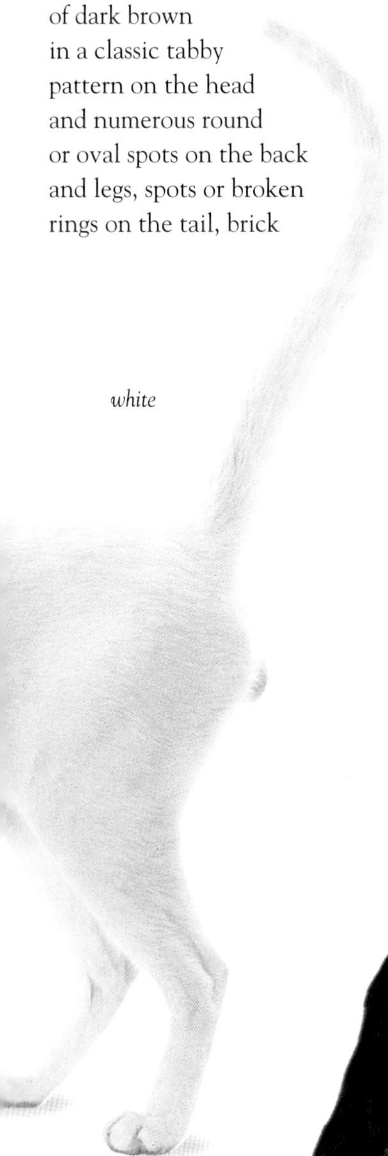

blue

Persian

The most popular breed of all in the U.S., the Persian is prized for its luxurious flowing coat, neat, pretty little face and sweet personality. It now comes in so many patterns and colors that it is almost impossible to choose a favorite.

copper-eyed white kitten

blue cream

HISTORY

The long coat of the original Persian was probably a mutation that developed spontaneously to cope with a cold climate, but since this cat became known in Europe in the 1600s, its beauty has been the spur to perfecting it. It is believed that the Persian was among the first breeds to be registered and shown, along with the Manx, Abyssinians and Domestic Shorthairs. Originally, they were called Longhairs rather than Persians, and this term was used until the early 1960s in the U.S. In Britain, they still go by the name Longhairs, and each color is considered a separate breed and may have a slightly different standard.

Today's U.S. Persian came about from matings between the Angora and the Maine Coon cats. The early influence of the Maine Coon is still very apparent on the show bench, with many silver and tabby Persians retaining the larger and higher-set ears of that ancestor. With selective breeding and crossing only like colors, great advances were made in the setting of the Persian type. Many of the outstanding blues produced in Britain in the 1940s and 1950s eventually became the breeding stock of catteries in the U.S. These blues are still considered the yardstick by which every other color is judged, and any blue Persian being exhibited must meet or excel in its standard.

DESCRIPTION

The ideal Persian is a medium to large cat with a broad, stocky body, cobby in type and low on the legs. The chest is broad and deep, the shoulders and rump equally wide across, with a

cream

well-rounded mid-section. The muscles are firm and well developed. The head is broad and well rounded when viewed from any angle. The forehead is domed with no vertical ridges. The cheeks are full and the nose is short, snub and broad. There is a decided horizontal indentation between the eyes, called the break. The chin is full and well developed in profile, with the chin, nose and forehead in a perpendicular line. The jaws are broad and powerful and the neck is so short and thick that it looks as if the head is sitting directly on top of the shoulders.

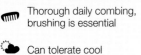

PET FACTS

🐾 Thorough daily combing, brushing is essential

☁️ Can tolerate cool climate

🐈 Double coat, very long, dense, thick, lively

🐈 Loving companions, calm, gentle, relatively quiet

🐾 **DID YOU KNOW?**
Although they may look helpless, Persians can be able hunters.

chocolate

red

The eyes are large, round, brilliant, set level and far apart, and the color must conform to the coat color. The eyes should be cleaned daily as part of the grooming routine. The ears are small, round-tipped, tilted forward and set wide apart. They should not be unduly open at the base, and should fit closely into the rounded contour of the head.

The legs are short, thick and straight with heavy boning. The feet are firm and well rounded, and long tufts between the toes are desirable. The paw pads should harmonize with the coat color. The tail is in proportion to body length, with considerable fullness.

The thick coat can be up to 6 inches (15 cm) long, and is soft, dense and full of life. There should be a long, full ruff. The main drawback is that the coat must be groomed every day because it sheds year-round and the cat will have problems with matting and hairballs if the dead hair is not removed regularly. Use a metal comb or a brush with long wires or natural bristles for the task. Many owners like to bathe their animals, and there are specific instructions for the care of different colors and coat types for show purposes. Learn the tricks from enthusiasts at shows and from professional groomers.

VARIETIES

In Britain, each Longhair color has a slightly different standard for head and body type. In the U.S., all colors of Persians must compete to the same exacting dictates of the standard, which puts some colors at a disadvantage. It is not as easy to produce a silver Persian with the same head type and ear set as most of the other colors. In the U.S., pointed colors are called Himalayan Persians in most associations, although in some they are still classified solely as Himalayans and judged as a separate breed. In Britain, they are called Colorpoint Longhairs.

black smoke

shaded cameo

chinchilla silver

tortoiseshell

red and white

As well as being classified by color, Persians are further separated into divisions in each of which most of the colors can be found. The solid division comprises the whites (blue-eyed, copper-eyed and odd-eyed), creams, blacks, blues, reds, lilacs and chocolates. All, except the whites, must have brilliant copper eyes.

The star of the shaded division is the chinchilla silver. This is a pure white cat with delicate black tipping on the ends of the hairs, brick red nose leather, and blue-green eyes. In the U.S., there is also a Shaded Silver class that calls for heavier black tipping and dark mascara markings on the face, but in Britain, there is only one class of silvers. Other lovely colors in the shaded division include

goldens, cameos (white cats with red tipping), as well as chinchilla and shaded versions of all of the solid colors. Eyes must be copper, except for the silvers with blue-green eyes, and the goldens with green to hazel eyes.

Next comes the smoke division, with such colors as cream smoke, black smoke, blue smoke, cameo smoke, lilac smoke, chocolate smoke and tortoiseshell smoke. This class calls for a solid white cat so heavily tipped on its outer hair with one of the above colors that it looks like a solid colored cat. The breathtaking beauty of the smoke is apparent when you blow softly down the back and the hair parts to reveal the snowy white undercoat. The smoke usually has copper eyes and a luxurious white ruff framing its face.

The tabby division consists of cream tabby, brown tabby, blue tabby, red tabby, chocolate tabby, lilac tabby, silver tabby, cameo tabby and torbie (patched tabby). Each of these comes in four

tabby patterns, classic (or blotched), ticked, mackerel or spotted. The tabby patterns should be clearly distinguishable from the ground color and, except for the silver tabby, all eye color must be copper. These cats are quite striking in appearance.

The tortoiseshell division is the smallest and is composed of blue creams, lilac creams, chocolate creams and tortoiseshell (red and black). The pattern is comprised of the two colors randomly splotched over the cat. A dividing mark

down the nose and under the chin (called a "blaze") is desirable. The eyes should be copper colored.

The particolor (also called bicolor) division is made up of calicos—a white cat with red and black splotches—that are also called tortoiseshell and white, as well as a lilac calico, a blue calico, a chocolate calico, and any of the solid, smoke, tortoiseshell, shaded or tabby colors with the addition of white. The

brown classic tabby

tortie point Himalayan

calico

TEMPERAMENT

Calm and gentle, the Persian is a lovable and appealing animal. It is hard to resist that little face, almost lost in fur, and fortunately, this cat enjoys being admired, petted and pampered. It will pose, draping itself on a windowsill or chair almost like a piece of art. It has a quiet, melodious voice and responds to stroking with delighted little chirps and murmurs. The large eyes are also most expressive of contentment. The Persian enjoys company but is not demanding in this respect and is quite capable of entertaining itself while you are out of the house for a few hours without tearing the place apart. It has a quality of great stillness and serenity and will sometimes sit for long periods doing absolutely nothing except looking beautiful.

eyes should be a brilliant copper to orange color.

The newest division (in most associations) is the Himalayan. This covers colorpoint Persians that are lilac point, blue point, chocolate point, seal point, red point, tortie point and lynx point. The tortie and lynx points may be seal, blue, lilac or chocolate. All Himalayans must have blue eyes.

chocolate point Himalayan

blue cream point Himalayan

Ragdoll

The Ragdoll is so named because of its ability to relax totally, like a ragdoll, when handled. This, along with its intelligence, even temperament and devotion to its owners, makes the Ragdoll a great pet for families with children.

blue mitted

HISTORY

The Ragdoll was developed in California during the 1960s from a white longhair and a seal point Birman. Subsequently, Burmese was added to the mix. The breed has been surrounded in controversy ever since, and although recognized for championship showing in 1965, it has yet to achieve that status with the Cat Fanciers' Association (CFA), the largest cat association in the U.S. It has recently been recognized in Britain but not as yet in many other countries. One of the controversial claims made for the Ragdoll is that it does not feel pain, but this certainly has no basis. The Ragdoll's habit of lying relaxed and unprotesting when handled may have led to this misconception.

DESCRIPTION

The ideal Ragdoll has a large, well-boned, muscular and substantial body, somewhat elongated. It is massive across the shoulders and chest and heavy in the hindquarters with a tendency to develop a "fatty pad" (greater omentum) on the lower abdomen. The head is a broad modified wedge with the appearance of a flat plane between the ears. The medium-length muzzle is round, with a well-developed chin. The medium-length nose has a break between the eyes and the leather harmonizes with the coat. The neck is short, heavy and

strong. The eyes are sapphire blue, large and oval. They are wide set and in line with the base of the ear. The medium-sized ears are wide at the base with rounded tips. They are set to gently cup the skull and continue the wedge shape.

The strong-boned legs are medium to medium-long, with the back legs longer than the front. The fur on the front legs is short and thick, while that on the hind legs is medium to long, thick and feathery. The paws are large, round and feather-

seal bicolor

PET FACTS

- Daily combing and brushing
- Can cope with a cool climate
- Semi-long to long, plush
- Affectionate, gentle and tolerant

DID YOU KNOW?

The Ragdoll's color, as with all colorpointed cats, is not fully developed until it is about two years old, and the cat continues to grow until it is about four years of age.

seal mitted

tufted with pad colors that harmonize with the coat. The tail is long, fluffy and in proportion to body length.

The plush, silky coat is medium-long to long, being longest around the neck and outer edges of the face. Although the fur is non-matting, the coat must be combed daily with a wide-toothed comb to remove tangles and dead hair, then brushed gently with a long-bristled brush. This is especially important at the end of winter as the weather warms and the heavy coat is shed, to reduce the possibility of hairballs forming.

seal point

VARIETIES

The Ragdoll is a colorpointed cat and comes in lilac point, blue point, chocolate point and seal point in each of three patterns—colorpoint, mitted and bicolor. The CFA will accept only the bicolor for championship showing, while some other associations have added the colors of red point, tortie point and lynx point.

TEMPERAMENT

Known for its loving and adaptable nature, the Ragdoll quickly becomes attached to its owner. It is gentle, intelligent and even-tempered.

Russian Blue

Handsome, gentle and sweet natured, the Russian Blue is in every way a classic. Its elegant lines, astonishingly rich coat and striking green eyes always turn heads, and, added to all that, it is healthy and easy to look after.

four-month-
old kitten

HISTORY

The breed seems to have originated in the most northerly regions of Russia and Scandinavia and went by a variety of names, including Archangel cats, Foreign blues, Spanish cats and Maltese cats, the reasons for which have long been forgotten. The Maltese cat label persisted in the U.S. until early this century. A Russian Blue competed in Britain in 1875 in a class for all-blue cats of all types, but it was not until 1912 that the breed was separated into a class of its own. Little work was done with the Russian Blue until after World War II, when American breeders combined the British bloodlines, with their plush, silvery coats, with Scandinavian strains, with their emerald-green eyes and flat profiles. The flat profiles came from crosses of a blue cat from Finland with a blue point Siamese.

DESCRIPTION

The lithe, slender and graceful Russian Blue has a fine-boned body that is firm, muscular and long, but not tubular. The head is a medium wedge, neither long and tapering nor short and massive. The muzzle is blunt and part of the total wedge. The top of the skull is long and flat in profile, gently descending to slightly above the eyes and continuing at a slight downward angle in a straight line to the tip of the nose. The nose leather is slate gray in the U.S. and blue in the Britain. There is no nose break or stop, but the thick fur of some animals makes it seem that there is a slight dip in the nose when light is reflected off the silver tipping. The face is broad.

PET FACTS	
🪮	Daily hand grooming
☁	Can tolerate cool climate
🐈	Short, dense, plush
🐈	Undemanding, intelligent and affectionate

🐾 **DID YOU KNOW?**
The Russian emperor Czar Nicholas II doted on his pet Russian Blue called Vashka.

186

The wide-set eyes are rounded and vivid green and the wide-set ears are rather large and broad at the base, with tips more pointed than rounded, and with a slight flare.

The fine-boned legs are long and the paws small and slightly rounded with pads of lavender pink or mauve in the U.S. and blue in Britain. The tapered tail is long and in proportion to the body. The double coat is short, dense, fine and plush, like seal fur. No other cat has a coat quite like it. It stands out from the body and has a distinctive soft and silky feel. The ideal coat will hold the imprint of your fingers as you run them through it. Grooming entails regular hand grooming and an occasional combing or a rub with a damp chamois to bring up the luster.

VARIETIES
The Russian Blue is shown only in blue. Lighter shades are preferred and the color should be even and bright throughout and free from tabby markings. The guard hairs are distinctly tipped with silver, giving the cat a lustrous, silvery shine.

TEMPERAMENT
Docile and affectionate, the Russian Blue quickly becomes devoted to its loved ones. It is gentle, playful and a good companion. Although somewhat shy, it gets along well with children and other pets. It is very intelligent and likes to fetch and open doors. It has a quiet, almost musical little voice.

Scottish Fold

The unusual ears of this gentle cat can give it the inquiring and charming look of a barn owl. Although not the result of a deliberate crossing, the Scottish Fold has already become one of the ten most popular cats in the U.S.

HISTORY
Although kittens with this type of genetic mutation have probably been appearing for a long time, the first Fold we know anything about was discovered in the litter of a farm cat near Coupar Angus in the Tayside Region of Scotland in 1961. She was a white cat named Susie. All of today's Folds are Susie's descendants.

Two Folds should never be bred together because of the danger of rigidity of the tail and stiffness in the hind legs in the kittens. Because Folds are often bred with American or British Shorthairs in the U.S. and with British Shorthairs in Britain, the two types are now distinctly different in head type and coat texture. The gene for the folded ears is dominant, so some kittens in each litter will have them, but not all. The breed is still unrecognized by the Governing Council of the Cat Fancy of Britain, but it has championship status with the Cat Association of Britain and was granted championship status in the U.S. in 1978.

DESCRIPTION
The stocky, medium-sized body is well padded, rounded and proportioned evenly from shoulder to pelvis. Preference in type seems to lean toward the British Shorthair crossing.

The head of this crossing is well rounded and the muzzle has well-rounded whisker pads; the head should blend into a short neck. The cheeks are prominent with a jowly appearance in the males. The large, well-rounded eyes are wide open with a sweet expression and are separated by a broad nose. Their color usually corresponds to the coat color. The broad nose is short with a gentle curve and a brief stop is permitted, although a definite nose break is a fault. The nose leather should match the coat color.

calico

five-week-old kittens

The ears are this cat's distinguishing feature and should fold forward and downward and sit like a cap on the rounded head. A smaller, tightly folded ear is preferred over one that is loosely folded and large. The ear tips are rounded.

There must be no hint of thickness in the legs or lack of mobility due to short, coarse legs. The paws are neat and round, with pads to harmonize with the coat color. The tapered tail is of medium length. When judging the Fold, the tail should be gently manipulated to make sure that it is flexible and not rigid.

The coat comes in both long and shorthaired versions and should be dense and resilient. Regular brushing will remove dead hair and keep the coat in good condition.

VARIETIES

The Scottish Fold comes in all colors and patterns, except solid lilac, chocolate and colorpointed.

PET FACTS	
🪮	Daily grooming
☁	Can tolerate a cool climate
🐈	Dense, plush
🐾	Quietly affectionate and well adjusted

🐾 **DID YOU KNOW?**
The Scottish Folds are no more prone to ear infections than cats with conventional ears.

TEMPERAMENT

With its mixture of British and American Shorthair ancestors, the Fold has the best traits of both breeds. It loves human companionship, is placid and very affectionate and easily adjusts to other pets. A hardy cat with a sweet disposition, it has a tiny voice and is not very vocal.

cream mackerel tabby

white

Selkirk Rex

A well-proportioned cat, the Selkirk Rex is being developed from a spontaneous genetic mutation that appeared only a decade ago. As yet, this good-natured cat is little known outside the U.S., but it seems certain to win hearts.

tortie point kitten, longhair

red classic tabby shorthair

resulting litter were curly coated, so it seems that the curls are associated with a dominant gene. Persians, Exotic Shorthairs and British and American Shorthairs are among the breeds that have contributed to the makeup of this attractive cat. Buyers should be aware, however, that this is still a very new breed, so genetic weaknesses associated with its genes may yet be discovered.

HISTORY

This is the most recent of the Rex variations to appear. The first cat with this naturally curled coat was found in 1987 in Wyoming, USA, and the type has already been accepted for championship competition by all U.S. associations. The original cat was crossed with a purebred black Persian and three of the six kittens in the

DESCRIPTION

The Selkirk Rex is being developed as a large, heavy-boned cat, rather like the British Shorthair in conformation. The substantial, muscular torso is rectangular and the back is straight. The shoulders and hips should be the same width. The head is round, broad and full-cheeked with no flat planes. In profile, the

nose has a stop or moderate break, and the nose leather is in harmony with the coat color. The chin is firm and well developed, and both male and female have definite jowls. The eyes are large, rounded and set well

red longhair

cream point shorthair

black smoke shorthair

PET FACTS

- Light regular combing
- Can tolerate cool weather
- Medium-long, soft, plush
- Sturdy and affectionate, extremely patient

DID YOU KNOW?
Selkirk Rex kittens lose their first curly coat. After it has been shed, coarse hair grows sparsely, eventually being replaced by the fully developed adult coat when they are about ten months old.

and lanky. The large paws are round and firm, with pads that harmonize with the coat color.

The coat is considerably longer than the other Rex breeds, with definite guard hairs. It is soft, plush, full and obviously curly, with the soft feel of lambswool. The hair is arranged in loose, individual curls that may be more evident around the neck, on the tail and on the belly. If the coat is combed every few days with a wide-toothed comb, it will remove dead hair and help the cat to maintain the coat in good condition. For

apart. The eye color need not conform to coat color. The medium-sized ears are pointed and set well apart.

The medium-length legs are well-boned, being neither short and cobby nor long

showing, spritz the coat with water between judgings to bring out the curl—this works better than combing. Too much combing and brushing of a wet coat will straighten the hairs and the curl will be less obvious.

VARIETIES
All colors and patterns are acceptable, including solid lilac, chocolate, tabby and colorpointed.

TEMPERAMENT
Healthy, sturdy and incredibly patient, the Selkirk Rex has a loving, tolerant disposition.

brown tabby longhair

Siamese

A gift fit for a king, the Siamese cat is a true aristocrat, with elegant lines and beautiful coloring. It can, however, be rowdy and boisterous, and it is perhaps this contradiction that makes the breed universally popular.

lilac point

chocolate point

HISTORY

The original Siamese cats, which are still to be found in Thailand, bear little or no resemblance to today's show types. They have stocky bodies, rounded heads, crossed eyes and kinked tails, all of which would disqualify them from competition today. In its native land, the Siamese was nurtured and protected within the temple and palace walls for centuries, and featured prominently in art and literature. The breed became known to the rest of the world when the royal family of Siam (now Thailand) presented them as gifts to visiting dignitaries. This was considered a great honor because the cats belonged exclusively to royalty.

The Siamese began appearing in British cat shows in the late nineteenth century and in America in the early part of this century. The only accepted color was seal point, and when blue points were introduced in

1934, some judges were so opposed to this new color that they refused to judge them as a separate class, which caused great consternation. The next color to be recognized, in 1946, was the chocolate point. This color resulted from a daughter of Wong Mau, the original Burmese imported into the U.S., being mated to a Siamese. In 1955, the lilac point (also known as the frost point) was recognized.

These four colors prevailed for a number of years until the breeders of red points, tortie points and lynx points began to clamor for recognition of their colors. The cat fancy was divided about whether to accept these latest colors. Debate raged, sometimes quite heatedly. As a result, some associations accepted red, tortie and lynx points as Siamese. Others accepted them as a separate breed called Colorpoint Shorthairs.

blue point

DESCRIPTION

The ideal Siamese is sleek, slender and refined in every respect. Its medium-sized body is graceful, long and svelte, combining fine bones and firm muscles. The shoulders and hips continue the tubular lines and the hips are never wider than the shoulders. The abdomen is tight and firm. The head is a long, tapering wedge, starting at the nose and flaring out in straight lines to the tips of the ears to form a triangle, with no break at the whiskers. The muzzle is fine and wedge-shaped. The tip of the chin lines up with the tip of the nose in the same vertical plane, neither receding nor excessively massive.

The almond-shaped eyes are medium sized and slant upward from the nose, following the line of the head and ears. They should not be crossed and any hint of a crossed eye is grounds for disqualification on the show bench. They are always brilliant sapphire blue, with deeper and more vivid shades being preferred. The ears are

seal tortie point

VARIETIES
Siamese are colorpoint cats and come in seal point, blue point, chocolate point, lilac point, red point, tortie point and lynx point. (The last three are called Colorpoint Shorthairs in the Cat Fanciers' Association.) The tortie and lynx points also come in lilac, blue, chocolate and seal.

Seal point: the body is an even warm cream, darker on the back and lighter on the stomach and chest; the points are seal brown; the nose leather and paw pads are seal brown.

Blue point: the body is an even bluish white with a warmer tone on the stomach and chest; the points, nose leather and paw pads are slate blue.

large, pointed and open at the base.

The legs are long and slim with dainty, small, oval paws. The long, thin tail tapers to a fine point and has no kinks.

All Siamese are shorthaired, but some associations now refer to the Balinese as a longhaired Siamese.

The Siamese coat is short, fine-textured and glossy, and lies close to the body. It can look as if it is "painted on." Grooming is minimal. Combing and brushing twice a week to remove dead hair will be quite sufficient. To make the coat gleam, wipe it over with a damp chamois.

blue lynx point

Chocolate point: the body is an even warm ivory all over; the points are warm milk chocolate; the nose leather and paw pads are cinnamon pink.

Lilac point: the body is glacial white (U.S.) or magnolia (Britain) all over; points are frosty gray with a pink or lilac tone; the nose leather and paw pads are lavender pink.

Red point: the body is pure white, shaded with the color of the points; the points are apricot to deep red, with the deeper shades preferred; the nose leather and paw pads are flesh or coral pink.

Tortie point: the colors of the coat, nose leather and paw pads are as above for seal, blue, chocolate and lilac points, but within the color is a tabby pattern. Irregular patches of red and/or cream on the points; red and/or cream mottling on the ears and tail is permitted.

Lynx point: the colors of the coat, nose leather and paw pads are as above for seal, blue, chocolate and lilac points, but within the color is a striped pattern.

blue cream point

TEMPERAMENT

The Siamese is intelligent and lovable. It will continually amuse you with its antics while occasionally frustrating you with its ability to open seemingly locked cupboards and doors. It is a people cat and demands attention— the Siamese hates to be ignored or left by itself, and can be mischievous if bored or lonely. These cats communicate like no other. The voice of the Siamese is legendary—a female in season sounds exactly like a baby wailing for its mother and can be easily heard a block away. One of the more highly strung breeds, agile and active and seeming to be in perpetual motion, it is not the cat for everyone. But for those who take this boisterous cat into their home, the reward is boundless affection and hours of entertainment.

red point

seal point kitten

chocolate point kitten

Siberian

A magnificent, wild-looking cat, the Siberian is an excellent hunter and is well adapted to surviving in a climate of extreme temperatures. Little is known of its background, but some people think that it is one of the earliest longhaired breeds.

PET FACTS

- Light regular grooming
- Can tolerate cool climate
- Long, dense, thick
- Hardy and loving companions

DID YOU KNOW?
The Siberian is Russia's native cat. It has been bred there for more than 1,000 years.

cream mackerel tabby

DESCRIPTION
A large, strong, well-muscled cat, the Siberian differs from the Maine Coon and Norwegian Forest cats in that the general impression is one of roundness and circles rather than wedges and angles. Its body is moderately long and substantial, with the back slightly curved or arched. The mature body should have an overall sausage shape with tight muscles and large bones.

The head is a modified wedge of medium size with well-rounded contours, broader at the skull and narrowing slightly to a full, rounded muzzle and a well-rounded chin. The cheekbones are neither set high nor prominent. The top of the head is flat and the nose curves slightly in a gentle slope. The nose pad is a color that harmonizes with the coat. The eyes are large, expressive and almost round. They are set wide with the

HISTORY
Siberian Forest Cats are not common outside Russia, but in their homeland, they are an ancient breed. The first cats of this breed were imported to the U.S. from Russia in 1990 and they are already attracting a great deal of attention. They have also been shown in championship competition in Europe. At present, they are not accepted in the U.S. by the Cat Fanciers' Association, although they can be shown in the other associations.

brown tabby

outer corner angled toward the inner base of the ear. Although the eyes are usually golden-green, any eye color is allowed and it need not conform to the coat color. The medium-large ears are broad at the base and set far apart. Tufts of hair on the tips of the ears are desirable.

The legs are moderately long with heavy bones. The paws are large and rounded and toe tufts are desirable. The paw pads are a color in keeping with the coat. The tail is medium length, wide at the base and blunt at the tip, with abundant hair.

On the body, the double coat is moderately long to long, with a dense, paler undercoat and full ruff. The thick coat is quite specialized to protect the animal from extremes of cold in its native land and the oily guard hairs make it water resistant and able to shed snow easily. The coat does not mat, but light, regular grooming is recommended, especially during spring and summer, when the heavy winter coat is shed. This will help to prevent hairballs.

brown mackerel tabby

VARIETIES

The Siberian cat comes only as a longhair. Although brown tabby is the most common color, it may be any pattern or color or combination of colors, except colorpoint, solid lilac or solid chocolate. The longer hairs are pale near the skin, darkening toward the outer end. This makes the coat shimmer as the cat moves.

TEMPERAMENT

The Siberian cat has a sweet personality to go with the sweet expression on its face. It is robust, and makes a loving, gentle and faithful companion.

cream tabby

Singapura

Small and beautifully proportioned, the Singapura is a recent arrival on the U.S. show scene and its rarity has perhaps enhanced the myths that surround it. It is an extremely pretty cat that enjoys wide appeal.

HISTORY

While its origin remains shrouded in mystery, the foundation stock of all Singapuras in the U.S. is just four cats belonging to a single American breeder. They are reputed to have a connection with Singapore street cats, but this is far from certain. Whatever the truth, the gene pool is small and the future of these cats is questionable.

The breed is being developed in the U.S. and it was first accorded championship status in 1988. It then went on to win 22 grand championship titles in its second season of showing, an amazing success.

DESCRIPTION

This is a small cat with a delicate coloring unlike any other breed. It has a moderately stocky, muscular body, and when the animal is standing, the body, legs and floor form a square. The neck is short and thick and the head is rounded with a blunt, medium-short nose. There is a definite whisker break. In profile, there is a slight stop well below eye level; the nose then continues in a straight line to the chin. The nose leather is salmon pink, outlined with dark brown. The large, almond-shaped eyes are held wide open and are outlined with dark brown. They slant slightly upward at the outside end. No eye color except hazel, green or yellow is permitted. Brilliance is preferred and small eyes are a serious fault.

adult with kittens

PET FACTS

🪮 Occasional combing

☁ Needs a warm climate

🐈 Very short, fine

🐾 Affectionate and playful

🐾 **DID YOU KNOW?**
The Singapura is the smallest breed of cat. Its name is Malaysian for Singapore.

The ears are large and slightly pointed, wide open at the base and deeply cupped. They should have a definite covering of light hair inside. Small ears are considered a serious fault.

The legs are heavy and well-muscled and taper to small, short oval feet and the paw pads are rosy brown. The tail, darker than the rest of the coat, is slender but not whip-like and has a blunt tip. It should have no kinks.

The sleek, silky coat feels like satin. It is fine, very short, and lies very close to the body—a springy coat is a fault. It needs little grooming beyond an occasional combing. The sepia coat color is unique. The ground color is old ivory, with each hair on the back, top of the head, and flanks ticked with at least two bands of a deep brown separated by bands of warm old ivory (this is also known as agouti ticking). The underside of the body is a lighter shade, like unbleached muslin.

VARIETIES

The Singapura comes only as a shorthair and only in sepia, with ticked fur.

TEMPERAMENT

Active, curious and quietly affectionate, the Singapura loves to be with people. It remains interactive and playful even when fully grown and gets along remarkably well with other animals. It is a speedy and effective hunter and the queens are noted for being particularly maternal and loving.

Snowshoe

While still comparatively rare, this hybrid of the Siamese and the bicolor American Shorthair has all the good points of its forebears. The prettily marked Snowshoe is lively, affectionate and very responsive to humans.

HISTORY

Seal points and blue points with white boots, throats and facial markings have occurred spontaneously for decades. But one group of dedicated breeders in the U.S. was so taken with the distinctive white patterning of such kittens, that they worked for years from the late 1960s to set a standard and to have these cats accepted as a new breed, which they called the Snowshoe. This cat is the result of crossings of Siamese, Birman and bicolor American Shorthairs. It was registered by the Cat Fanciers' Federation and the American Cat Association by 1974 and gained championship status in 1982, but not all associations recognize it for championship status yet.

DESCRIPTION

The Snowshoe combines the heftiness of its domestic Shorthair ancestors with the body length of its oriental ancestors. It has an athletic appearance of great power and agility, like a runner. The medium-sized body is rectangular, well muscled, powerful and heavily built. The neck should be of medium length. The head is a slightly rounded triangular wedge, with cheekbones set

blue point

high. The medium-length nose is straight with a slight rise on the bridge. The nose leather varies with coat color. The large, round eyes are a vivid blue and should slant up from the nose toward the base of each ear. The medium-sized ears are slightly rounded at the tips and set forward from the outside of the head giving a continuing line from the head to the ears.

The strong, well-muscled legs should be of good length, in proportion to the body and well boned, but not as heavy as those of the American Shorthair. The medium-length tail should taper to a point.

The glossy coat is short to medium length and should not be double or plush. The ideal pattern, which is quite a challenge to produce, calls for a solid color on the back and sides of the animal with white confined to the insides of the legs and belly. A white throat is desirable as is white on the underside of the head. The preferred facial pattern is a white muzzle in the shape

seal point

VARIETIES
Preference is for cats displaying the proper amount of white and in the preferred pattern. Only two colors are allowed— seal point or blue point. The nose leather and paw pads may be either pink or the color of the points or a combination of the two.

TEMPERAMENT
Lively and adaptable, the Snowshoe combines the best characteristics of its American Shorthair, Birman and Siamese ancestors, and is an excellent hunter. It is full of fun, a good companion and gets along well with other animals. It becomes quite devoted to its owner.

of an inverted "V." Preferred foot markings are matching white boots extending to the bend of the ankle on the front feet, and matching white boots extending to just below the hock on the back feet. Only minimal grooming is required—an occasional combing to remove dead hair will suffice.

seal point

seal point

Somali

With its beautiful coat of many colors, the agile Somali is enjoying a roller-coaster ride to fame and popularity. It makes a delightful and entertaining pet.

History

A longhaired version of the Abyssinian, the Somali was developed from longhaired kittens that appeared in the litters of Abyssinians carrying the gene for long hair. (Somalis, conversely, never produce shorthaired kittens.) The Somali Cat Club of America was founded in 1972 and recognition for championship showing was soon gained from the now-defunct National Cat Fanciers' Association. Somalis are now accepted for championship showing in all U.S. associations and are becoming increasingly popular throughout the world, although not all of the glorious coat colors are accepted for show purposes.

PET FACTS

- Daily brushing
- Can tolerate cool weather
- Semi-long, dense
- Playful, active and needs human companionship

DID YOU KNOW?
The name Somali was chosen for this cat because of its close relationship to the Abyssinian. Somalia and Abyssinia (present-day Ethiopia) are next-door neighbors.

ruddy

Description

The medium-long body is lithe and graceful with strong, well-developed muscles. The rib cage is rounded and the back is slightly arched, which makes it look as if the cat is about to spring. Its structure strikes a balance between cobby and svelte.

blue

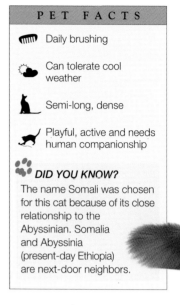

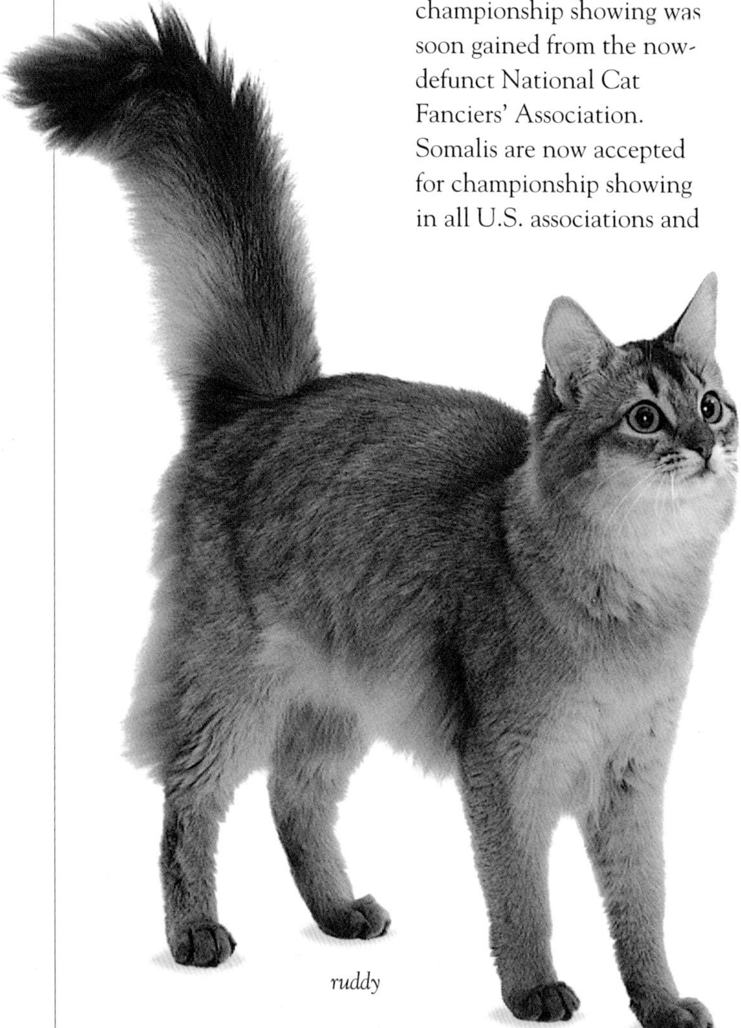

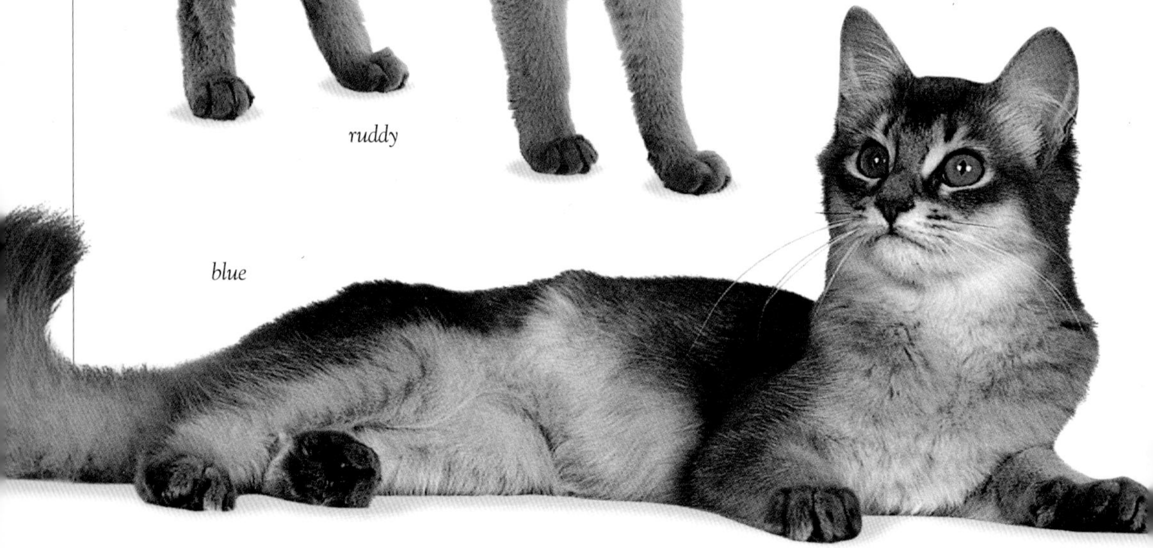

red

The legs are in proportion to the torso and the oval feet are small, with tufted toes. The paw pads vary with the coat color. The tail has a full brush, is thick at the base and tapers to a slender tip.

The double, medium-length coat is very soft, extremely fine and the denser the better. It doesn't mat, but should be combed regularly to remove dead hair. Preference is given to those cats with a ruff and britches, giving a full-coated appearance. Any white must be confined to the upper throat, chin or nostrils.

VARIETIES

The Somali comes in red, ruddy, blue and fawn. The hair is ticked everywhere, except on the underside of the body, but the ticking is not fully developed until the cat is about 18 months old. Each hair may have as many as three distinct bands. The chest, inside of the legs and belly must be clear of markings. A faint broken necklace, although not desirable, is acceptable. A dark unbroken necklace would cause disqualification in a show specimen.

TEMPERAMENT

Intelligent, extroverted and very sociable, the Somali has a zest for life, loves to play, and thrives on human companionship. It likes to spend time outdoors and may be restless if confined. It has a soft voice, but is not usually very vocal.

The head is a modified, slightly rounded wedge, without flat planes; the brow, cheek and profile lines all showing a gentle contour. The almond-shaped eyes are large, brilliant and expressive, either gold, green or hazel, with deeper shades preferred. They are accented by dark lids and above each eye is a short, dark vertical stroke; dark horizontal strokes continue from the upper lid toward the ear. The large, moderately pointed ears are broad and cupped at the base. They are medium-set toward the back of the head. The inner ear should have horizontal tufts that reach nearly to the other side of the ear and tufts on the tips of the ears are desirable.

fawn

Sphynx

There seem to be no in-betweens with this cat—because of its appearance people either love it or hate it. One thing not in dispute, though, is that the Sphynx is the most unusual of cats. It is also very intelligent with a playful and affectionate nature.

blue and white

brown mackerel tabby

HISTORY
In the early 1900s, a cat resembling a modern-day Sphynx was exhibited as the New Mexican Hairless cat. Efforts to gain recognition for this breed were not made until hairless cats appeared in Ontario, Canada, in the 1960s. In 1970, it was granted provisional status by the Cat Fanciers' Association (CFA), but progressed no further because the CFA board was concerned that the breed might have genetic problems.

The Sphynx is currently accepted in the U.S. by only two of the associations—the American Cat Association and The International Cat Association. Breeders of today's Sphynx claim that in the cats now being bred there are no genetic flaws, but the cat is rarely seen outside the U.S. It has a higher than usual body temperature and needs to eat a little more than average to fuel its metabolism.

black

DESCRIPTION
The medium-length body is very sturdy and rounded, thick through the abdomen, with the appearance of having a full belly, but not fat. The chest is broad and barrel-shaped. The head is slightly longer than it is wide with prominent cheekbones and a slight but definite whisker break. The profile has a distinct stop at the bridge of the nose,

black and white kittens

PET FACTS

Daily sponging

Warm climates; cannot tolerate exposure to direct sunlight

Extremely short, fine

Playful and affectionate

DID YOU KNOW?
The Sphynx must always be protected against sunburn as the coat is not substantial enough to screen out the sun's harmful rays.

and the nose is covered with velvety fur. The neck is long and slender. The large eyes are deep-set and slant up toward the outer edge of the ear. Any eye color is acceptable and it need not conform to the coat color. The ears are very large, wide at the base and open, with no interior hair. They are upright, neither low-set nor on top of the head. The legs are long and slender, but not fine boned, and feel firm and muscular. The neat oval paws have long slender toes. The pads are a color in keeping with the coat. The tail is long, hard and tapered, with no kinks.

Despite appearances, the Sphynx is not really hairless. The skin is covered with very short, fine down that is almost imperceptible to both the eye and the hand. It should feel like soft suede. On the points (ears, muzzle, tail and feet) there is short, tightly packed soft hair. Lack of an insulating coat means that the cat feels quite warm when you touch it. Whiskers and eyebrows may be present, either whole or broken, or there may be none. The skin often has a wrinkled appearance, especially in kittens. Because these cats sweat, a most unusual trait, they should be sponged over daily with a damp sponge to remove oils.

VARIETIES
All Sphynx must conform to the coat description above. They can be any color and pattern, including colorpoint. Because of the invisibility of the hair, the pattern and color seem almost to be tatooed on the skin.

TEMPERAMENT
The Sphynx exudes quiet contentment. It has a surprising, mystical effect on anyone holding it for the first time, almost as if it casts a spell over the person. Owners claim that it is the most intelligent and affectionate of breeds.

brown mackerel torbie

Tonkinese

Beautiful soft colors characterize the luxurious coat of the Tonkinese, a cat with some of the best qualities of each of its parent breeds. The result of clever breeding, this lovely cat certainly justifies the effort made to create it.

platinum mink

HISTORY

The only breed to originate in Canada, the Tonkinese was developed in the early 1960s by crossing a seal point Siamese and a sable Burmese. Feeling that Siamese show types were becoming too stylized and extreme for popular taste, the breeder hoped to create a cat with some of the qualities she liked best in each breed. She believed the Tonkinese, especially those with points and blue eyes, would appeal to people searching for a Siamese of the more old-fashioned style.

A New York pet-store owner had been working toward the same goal about ten years earlier. He had called his cats Golden Siamese and the Canadian strain took the same name until it was changed to Tonkinese. The Tonkinese was first accepted for

natural mink

championship competition by the Canadian Cat Association in 1965 and in the U.S. in 1972. It is now registered with all U.S. associations, but not in all colors and patterns. In Britain, only one association accepts the breed and it allows all the standard recognized Burmese colors. Other countries have yet to appreciate the qualities of this delightful animal.

PET FACTS

- Occasional combing
- Needs warm climate
- Medium-short, fine
- Inquisitive, active, loving and responsive

DID YOU KNOW?

The Tonkinese doesn't always breed true. Only about half of the kittens of two Tonkinese parents will be true to type, which is the reason it is not accepted by some British associations.

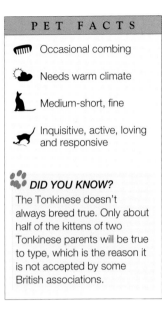

blue mink

champagne mink

DESCRIPTION

The ideal body shape is intermediate between the Siamese and Burmese, neither cobby nor svelte. It is medium sized with well-developed muscles.

The abdomen should be taut, well muscled and firm. The head is a modified wedge, somewhat longer than it is wide, with high, gently planed cheekbones. The muzzle is blunt and as long as it is wide. There is a slight whisker break and a slight stop at eye level. There is a gentle rise from the tip of the nose to the stop and a slight rise from the nose stop to the forehead. The nose leather should harmonize with the coat color.

The open, almond-shaped eyes slant up along the cheekbones toward the outer edges of the ears. Their striking aquamarine to turquoise color is a definitive characteristic of the Tonkinese breed and is seen at its best in natural light. They are the result of combining the blue of the Siamese with the gold of the Burmese. The medium-sized ears are covered with very short hair, and are broad at the base with oval tips. They are set as much on the sides of the head as on the top.

The legs are fairly slim and in proportion in length and boning to the body. The paws are more oval than round and the pads should harmonize with the coat color. The long tail tapers to a slender tip and should have no kinks.

The lustrous coat is medium-short in length, fine and silky, and lies close to the body. In the mature animal, the body color should be rich, even and unmarked, shading to a lighter tone on the underparts of the body. There must be a distinct contrast between body color and points, which may darken with age. The points are densely marked on the mask, ears, feet and tail. An occasional combing to remove dead hair, a brush with a rubber brush and a rub over with a damp chamois is all that is needed to keep the coat in good condition.

VARIETIES
Some associations allow other colors, like Siamese (pointed, with blue eyes) or Burmese (solid colored, with golden eyes), but the Tonkinese comes in only these five colors for championship showing in the U.S., either pointed or in solid colors:

Blue mink: the body is soft blue to blue-gray; the points are slate blue; the nose leather and paw pads are blue-gray.

Champagne mink: the body is soft, buff cream; the points are medium brown; the nose leather and paw pads are cinnamon brown.

Honey mink: the body is golden cream, preferably with an apricot cast; the points are light to medium ruddy brown; the nose leather and paw pads are caramel pink.

Natural mink: the body is medium brown; the points are dark brown; the nose leather and paw pads are dark brown.

Platinum mink: the body is pale, silvery gray with warm overtones; the points are frosty gray; the nose leather and paw pads are lavender pink.

champagne mink

natural mink

208

TEMPERAMENT
Intelligent, lively and lovable, the Tonkinese is in every way a charmer, with the strong personality and curiosity of the Siamese evident. It dislikes being left alone for long periods of time and can be mischievous if bored or lonely. If you must be absent for hours at a time, consider acquiring two cats so they can keep each other company. Make sure your home is escape-proof before you bring your Tonkinese home as it is adept at finding ways to get out. It is playful, affectionate, healthy, long-lived and easy to look after—what more could you ask?

blue mink

platinum mink

Turkish Angora

A cat with the most luxurious appearance, the ravishing Turkish Angora can truly be called a Turkish delight. One of the oldest longhaired breeds, strenuous efforts are being made in its homeland to maintain the purity of its bloodlines.

blue

black and white bicolor

HISTORY

The Turkish Angora is a pure, natural breed, probably domesticated by the Tartars. These cats became established in Turkey, where they were, and still are, highly regarded. In the sixteenth century, they were presented as gifts to European nobility by Turkish sultans. Since the 1940s, they have been a protected species and the Ankara Zoo has maintained a breeding colony of Angora cats, breeding only white cats. Although Angoras were known as far back as the 1890s, the Turkish Angora as we know it today did not reach the U.S. until 1962, when two were imported from Turkey's Ankara Zoo.

red classic tabby

DESCRIPTION

The ideal Turkish Angora is a lithe, balanced, graceful animal with a muscular, medium-sized body—overall balance and fineness of bone are more important than size. The torso is long and slender and the shoulders are the same width as the hips. The small to medium head is wedge-shaped, with a long, gently pointed nose. The nose leather is pink in the white Angora and should harmonize with the coat in other colors. The neck is long and slim. No break or hint of a break is allowed in the line of the nose. The large, almond-shaped eyes slant up slightly and have an open expression. The eyes can be any color with no relationship between eye color and coat color. White cats with odd eyes are prized because of their rarity. The large ears are wide at the base, pointed and tufted. They are set high on the head, vertical and erect.

The legs are long and sturdy, with small, round, dainty toes, preferably with tufts of hair in between. The paw pads are pink in the white Angora, but in keeping with the coat in other colors. The tail is long and plumed, tapering from a wide base to a narrow end.

The fine, dense, silky, medium-length coat shimmers with every movement. It is not fully developed until the cat is about two years old. There is no undercoat and the hair is mainly

210

straight, but wavy on the stomach. There is a long ruff and britches, with longer hair under the body than on the back. The coat should be combed regularly with a medium-toothed comb to remove dead hair and prevent matting. In order to avoid hairballs, grooming is very important during the spring when the winter coat is being shed.

VARIETIES

The original Turkish Angora was accepted only in white, with either blue, copper, green, amber or odd eyes. Although they are now registered in all colors and patterns, except colorpoint, solid lilac and chocolate, the majority of breeders still prefer to breed the original white cats.

TEMPERAMENT

Turkish Angoras make wonderful pets and are thought to be among the most intelligent of cat breeds. They are gentle and friendly, with great charm.

odd-eyed white

silver patched tabby and white

Turkish Van

The most unusual characteristic of the Turkish Van is that it has no reluctance to enter the water. It may have become so adapted because of a necessity to catch fish, but it now seems to swim for sheer pleasure, as many dogs do.

tortie and white

HISTORY
The founding members of the Turkish Van breed were two kittens taken to England from the Lake Van district in Western Turkey in 1955 by two British women on holiday there. They imported two more Van cats in 1959 and by 1969 the breed was accepted for championship competition in Britain. The following year, the first Vans officially arrived in the U.S. and they were registered there in 1985. Not all associations accept them yet for championship showing.

Although named after Lake Van, there is no evidence that the cats originated there. Armenian people who live around the lake and pronounce "Van" to rhyme with "Don," may have brought these swimming cats with them when they settled in the region.

DESCRIPTION
The Van is a solidly built cat with a very broad chest. Its strength and power are apparent in its thick-set body and legs. Mature males should exhibit marked muscular development in the neck and shoulders with the shoulders at least as broad as the head. There is a well-rounded ribcage and muscular hips. The head is a large, broad

PET FACTS

- Regular grooming
- Can tolerate cool climate
- Semi-long, soft, silky
- Agile, alert and companionable

DID YOU KNOW?
The aggressive nature of the Turkish Van has been tamed successfully by selective breeding. It is now quite a friendly animal.

calico

wedge, with gentle contours, a medium-length nose and prominent cheekbones. In profile, the nose has a slight dip below eye level. The nose leather is pink. The large, round eyes are slightly drawn out at the corners and set on a slant. They should be clear, alert and expressive and have pink rims. The moderately large ears are set fairly high and well apart. The tips are slightly rounded and the insides should be well feathered.

The legs are moderately long and muscular and set wide apart, tapering to rounded, somewhat large feet with tufts between the toes and pink paw pads. The tail is long, full and bushy.

The semi-longhaired coat has a texture like cashmere, soft to the roots with no trace of undercoat. For this reason, it dries quickly after the cat has been for a swim. There is feathering on the ears, legs, feet and belly. Facial fur is short, but there is a frontal neck

black and white

ruff that becomes more prominent with age. Combing twice a week to remove dead hair will keep the coat looking good, but give it extra attention when the heavy winter coat is being shed to avoid hairballs.

VARIETIES
The Turkish Van comes only in white, and in one pattern, van. This means that only the head and tail are colored and there can be no more than two spots on its body. The color may be solid, cream or auburn in Britain, but in the U.S., tabby and particolor are also allowed. A blaze or white streak up the nose to at least between the front edge of the ears is very desirable—to the Turks, it signifies the blessing of Allah.

TEMPERAMENT
This cat has an unusually melodious voice, is active and intelligent, and makes a lively companion to the right owner. It is not a lap-cat and will feel more secure, and handle better, with all four feet on a solid surface.

red and white

FURTHER INFORMATION

*When I observed he was a fine cat, saying,
"why yes, Sir, but I have had cats whom
I liked better than this"; and then as if
perceiving Hodge to be out of countenance,
adding, "but he is a very fine cat, a very
fine cat indeed."*

SAMUEL JOHNSON (1709-84),
English lexicographer

GLOSSARY

altered a cat that has had its reproductive organs removed (either spayed females or neutered males).

banding distinct bands of color in a cross-wise direction.

bay rum spirit a liquid, once made from bayberry leaves and now made from a mixture of oils, alcohol and water, helpful in removing stains.

bib the part of the ruff, or lengthened hair, around the chest area.

bicolor a cat with more than two spots of color on the torso, either white and one basic color, or white with one tabby color.

blaze a marking down the forehead, nose and under the chin.

boric-acid powder a white powder used as a mild antiseptic or preservative.

break an indentation at the bridge of the nose, between the eyes or just below the eyes. It is more visible than a stop.

britches long hairs on the back of the hind legs which run from the hips to the hock, or lower joint, of the leg.

calico van a white cat with two spots on the torso in two different basic colors.

cat fancier a person involved in breeding, selling and showing cats, usually pedigrees.

cat fancy the hobby of breeding, selling and showing cats, usually pedigreed cats.

cattery the place where a breeding cat is kept, either in the home or in a separate outbuilding.

cobby sturdy, round and compact body shape. The body is usually set low on the legs, with broad shoulders and rump.

colorpoint a cat with darker shadings on its mask, ears, paws and tail.

colostrum the milky fluid secreted from the mother's nipples, or mammary glands, for the first few days after birth. It is rich in protein and contains antibodies which help protect the young from disease.

cornstarch a fine powdery starch made from corn, rice or other grain. It is known as cornflour in Britain.

double coat a coat of double thickness. Unlike regular coats, the skin is not visible when the coat is parted.

euthanasia to put down, or cause death, in a painless and peaceful manner so as to end incurable illness and suffering.

feral cat an untamed domestic cat that was born, or has reverted to living in the wild.

flanks the fleshy sides of the cat between the ribs and the hips.

gene part of the chromosome from which hereditary traits are determined.

ground color the basic (or lighter) color of the cat in any of the tabby patterns.

guard hairs stiff, long, coarse, protective hairs that form a cat's outer coat.

hand grooming light stroking of the coat with your hand to remove dead hair.

hereditary traits/genes passed down from parents to offspring.

hock first, or lower, joint at the back of the legs.

household pet category name for mixed breeds in the US. If entering your mixed-breed cat in a show, he would be entered in this category.

in season period of time when the female, or queen, is willing to mate with the male, or studcat. Also referred to as estrus or "in heat."

inoculation the injection of a vaccine to create immunity. A small amount of a specific disease agent is injected enabling antibodies to build up to prevent the occurrence of the disease.

kink a twist, curl, bend or bump in the tail bone.

laces white markings on the legs.

locket solid white marking on the neck.

mackerel a type of tabby pattern where the colors of the coat appear striped.

mask the darker shadings on the face.

mineral spirits turpentine or paint thinner, helpful in removing stains.

mixed-breed a cat comprised of two or more different breeds, which do not combine to make a separate breed; not purebred.

mutation a variation in a genetic characteristic which is passed on to following generations. It is either accidental or environmental and can be either harmless or defective.

muzzle the jaws and mouth.

necklace bandings of color across the lower neck and chest area, as if the cat is actually wearing a necklace.

neuter to surgically remove the testicles of a male cat to prevent reproduction.

odd-eyed having different colored eyes, usually one eye is blue and the other is copper or yellow.

particolor comprising two colors, always white with one other basic color.

pedigree the line of direct descent or ancestry, or the certificate stating the descent or ancestry.

points extremities of the body comprising the mask, ears, legs and tail.

points (show) the score awarded to a cat depending on how the judge rates them according to the standard. A total of 100 points can be awarded by a judge.

pound rescue center or shelter for stray animals.

purebred a cat which has only been bred from cats of the same breed so as to produce the same characteristics and traits of previous generations.

quarantine the period of isolation to prevent the spread of a disease. Every country has its own regulations regarding the length of this period.

queen an unaltered female cat.

Roman nose nose with a lump on it.

rough-housing behaving in a boisterous, rough or rowdy manner.

ruff protruding or lengthened hair around the neck and chest.

spay to surgically remove the uterus and ovaries of a female cat to prevent reproduction.

spraying a natural instinctive act of urinating on surfaces as a means of marking territory. It is most common in the unaltered male cat but unaltered females and altered cats can still spray.

standards guidelines set out for each breed by all associations which list the qualities that the breed will be judged on in the show ring.

stop a slight indentation at the bridge of the nose, between the eyes or just below the eyes. It is not as visible as a break.

studcat an unaltered male cat, also known as a tomcat.

tabby patterned coat with circular, striped or blotchy markings.

tartar a hard, brownish deposit on the teeth that can cause decay.

ticked dark and light colors on the hair shaft, in alternate bands.

ticking light hairs that are scattered among darker colored hairs or spatterings of lighter hairs among darker colored hairs.

tomcat an unaltered male cat, also known as a studcat.

torbie a combination of the tortoiseshell and the tabby pattern that is also known by the name "patched tabby."

tortie abbreviation of tortoiseshell.

tortoiseshell a patched or mottled pattern that can resemble some turtles and tortoises.

unaltered an intact male or female with full reproductive abilities.

undercolor the color of the hair closest to the skin.

van having one or two spots on the torso. The spots are one of the basic colors.

walnut-shaped eyes eyes that are oval or almond-shaped on top and round on the bottom.

whisker break an indentation in the upper jaw.

whisker pads the thickened, or fatty pads around the whisker area.

INFORMATION DIRECTORY

The following organizations will be able to supply you with information on local contacts for details on registration, standards, cat shows and any other information required.

USA

American Cat Association
8101 Katherine Avenue
Panorama City CA 91402
Tel: 818 781 5656
Fax: 818 781 5340

Cat Fanciers' Association
PO Box 1005
Manasquan NJ 08736-0805
Tel: 732 528 9797
Fax: 732 528 7391

The International Cat Association
PO Box 2684
Harlingen TX 78551
Tel: 210 428 8046
Fax: 210 428 8047

American Cat Fanciers' Association
PO Box 203
Point Lookout MO 65726
Tel: 417 334 5430
Fax: 417 334 5540

Cat Fanciers' Federation
PO Box 661
Gratis OH 45330
Tel: 937 984 1841
Fax: 937 787 9009

CANADA

Canadian Cat Association
220 Advance B1 Ste 101
Bramptom Ontario L6T 4J5
Tel: 905 459 1481
Fax: 905 459 4023

EUROPE

Governing Council of Cat Fanciers
4–6 Penel Orlieu
Bridgewater
Somerset TA6 3PG
England
Tel: 01278 427575

Federation International Féline (FIFe)
General Secretary
Little Dene
Lenham Heath
Maidstone, Kent ME17 2BS
England
Tel: 01622 850913
Fax: 01622 850908

Cat Association of Britain (FIFe)
Mill House
Letcombe Regis
Oxon OX12 9JD
England
Tel: 01235 766543

AUSTRALIA

Royal Agricultural Society Cat Control of NSW
GPO Box 4317
Sydney NSW 2001
Tel: 02 9331 9132
Fax: 02 9331 5709

Feline Control Council of Victoria
Royal Showgrounds
Epsom Road
Ascot Vale VIC 3032
Tel: 03 9281 7404
Fax: 03 9376 2973

219

INDEX

CREDITS AND ACKNOWLEDGMENTS

PHOTOGRAPH CREDITS

(t = top; b = bottom;
c = centre; l = left; r = right
AA/ES = Animals Animals/Earth
Scenes; AA&AC = Ancient Art and
Architecture Collection; AD-LIB =
AD-LIBITUM; AU = Animals
Unlimited; Auscape = Auscape
International; BCI = Bruce Coleman
Incorporated - NYC; BCL = Bruce
Coleman Limited; Bridgeman =
The Bridgeman Art Library)

All photographs by Chanan
Photography except the following:

Banding by Stuart Bowey/AD-LIB,
except Chapter Five by Ferrero/
Labat/Auscape; chapter icons by
Stuart Bowey/AD-LIB; **cover**
Arrasmith McHale & Associates;
2 Nill/Silvestris 4-5 AU 6-7c
Bridgeman 8-9 Jane Burton/BCI
10-11c The American Museum in
Britain, Bath 12l The Iams Company
13t Hermeline/Cogis/Auscape; c Jane
Burton/BCL 14b Stock Image/
Austral International 15tl Vidal/
Cogis/Auscape; tr Stuart Bowey/
AD-LIB; b Stuart Bowey/AD-LIB
16tl Jane Burton/BCL 16-17b AU
17t Stuart Bowey/AD-LIB 18tl Sally
Anne Thompson/Animal
Photography 18-19b Jane Burton/
BCL 19t Sally Anne Thompson/
Animal Photography 20c Stuart
Bowey/AD-LIB 21t Jane Burton/
BCL; b Stuart Bowey/AD-LIB 22t
Stuart Bowey/AD-LIB; b David M
Barron/Oxygen Group/AA/ES 23t
M Grenet/A Soumillard/Pho.n.e/
Auscape; b AU 24t Labat/Cogis/
Auscape; b Renee Stockdale/AA/ES
25t Keith Ringland/Oxford Scientific
Films; b AU 26tl Stuart Bowey/
AD-LIB 27t Jane Burton/BCL;
b R Wilbie/Animal Photography
28-29 Victoria and Albert Museum/
Bridgeman 30t AU; b John Daniels/
Ardea London Ltd 31tl Richard
Packwood/Oxford Scientific Films;
r Stuart Bowey/AD-LIB 32 Stuart
Bowey/AD-LIB 33 Stuart Bowey/
AD-LIB 34 Stuart Bowey/AD-LIB
35 Stuart Bowey/AD-LIB 36t AU;

bl AU; br AU 37br Stuart Bowey/
AD-LIB 38t AU; b Hermeline/Cogis/
Auscape 39t Hermeline/Cogis/
Auscape; br AU; bl Stuart Bowey/
AD-LIB; bc Stuart Bowey/AD-LIB
40tl Hermeline/Cogis/Auscape;
b Stuart Bowey/AD-LIB 40-41b
Stuart Bowey/AD-LIB 41t AU;
c AU; b AU 42t AU; c AU; b AU
43c Jane Burton/BCL; b Stuart
Bowey/AD-LIB 44tl AU 44-45b
TSM - Peter Steiner/Stock Photos
45t Renee Stockdale/AA/ES; br AU
46 The Iams Company 47t The Iams
Company; cr Stuart Bowey/AD-LIB
48t Stuart Bowey/AD-LIB; b Stuart
Bowey/AD-LIB 48-49tc Stuart
Bowey/AD-LIB 49tr Sally Anne
Thompson/Animal Photography;
b AU 50tl Stuart Bowey/AD-LIB;
cl Stuart Bowey/AD-LIB;
bl M Grenet/A Soumillard/Pho.n.e/
Auscape 51tr Stuart Bowey/AD-LIB;
cr Stuart Bowey/AD-LIB; br AU
52-53c Private Collection/
Bridgeman 55t Stuart Bowey/
AD-LIB 56t Jane Burton/BCL
57b Sally Anne Thompson/Animal
Photography 59t AU; b Stuart
Bowey/AD-LIB 60b Jane Burton/
BCL 61t Lothar Lenz/Silvestris;
c Stuart Bowey/AD-LIB; b Stuart
Bowey/AD-LIB 62t Jane Burton/
BCL; b AU 63b AU 64b
W Rohdich/FLPA 67b AU;
r Francais/Cogis/Auscape 68tl
Hans Reinhardt/Pho.n.e/Auscape;
bl Francais/Cogis/Auscape 69t AU;
b Renee Stockdale/AA/ES 71t AU;
b Stuart Bowey/AD-LIB 72t Susanne
Danegger/Silvestris; b Gissey/Cogis/
Auscape 73t Hermeline/Cogis/
Auscape; c, b The Iams Company;
74t Jane Burton/BCL 75t John
Daniels/Ardea London Ltd; b Jane
Burton/BCL 76t Stuart Bowey/AD-
LIB; b Stuart Bowey/AD-LIB 77t
Stuart Bowey/AD-LIB; b Renee
Stockdale/AA/ES 78t Ralph
Reinhold/AA/ES 79 Stuart
Bowey/AD-LIB 80 b Jane
Burton/BCL 81b AU 83t Jane
Burton/BCL; b Sally Anne
Thompson/Animal Photography

84-85 Bonhams, London/Bridgeman
86-87b Jane Burton/BCL 86l AU
87tr Jane Burton/BCI 88t Harry
Ausloos/AA/ES 89t AU 90tl Jane
Burton/BCL; b Margaret Miller/
Photo Researchers 91t AU;
br M Grenet/A Soumillard/
Pho.n.e/Auscape 94t Jane Burton/
BCL; b Vidal/Cogis/Auscape 95b
Jane Burton/BCL 96tl AU; bl Jane
Burton/BCL; br Jane Burton/BCI 97t
Hans Reinhard/BCL ; bl Jane Burton/
BCI; br Jane Burton/BCI 98t
R Willbie/Animal Photography 99tl
M Grenet/A Soumillard/Pho.n.e/
Auscape;tr Stuart Bowey/AD-LIB;
b Stuart Bowey/AD-LIB 100t
Jean-Michel Labat/Pho.n.e./Auscape;
b Margot Conte/AA/ES 101t
M Grenet/A Soumillard/Pho.n.e/
Auscape 102-103c Private
Collection/Bridgeman 104c
Peter J. Green; b Renee Lynn/The
Photo Library, Sydney 105t Carol
Farneti-Foster/Planet Earth Pictures;
c James Carmichael/Image Bank;
b Francois Gohier/Ardea London Ltd
106tl Taronga Zoo; b Mark Deeble
& Victoria Stone/Oxford Scientific
Films 106-107t International
Photographic Library 107tr Alain
Dregesco/Planet Earth Pictures;
cr Kenneth W. Fink/Ardea London
Ltd; br Ferrero-Labat/Auscape 108l
Ronald Sheridan/AA&AC
108-109b British Museum 109tl
Ronald Sheridan/AA&AC; tr British
Museum 110tl Ronald Sheridan/
AA&AC; b National Gallery of Art,
Washington/Bridgeman 110-111tc
British Museum 111b Bonhams,
London/Bridgeman; cr Mary Evans
Picture Library 113tc Jean-Michel
Labat/Auscape; c Jean-Paul Ferrero/
Auscape 116-117c Abbazia Monte
Oliveto Maggiore/Scala 133t AU
136t Jean-Michel Labat/Auscape
159t Lanceau/Cogis/Auscape
214-215c Bonhams, London/
Bridgeman 216t Stuart Bowey/
AD-LIB 216-217b Stuart Bowey/
AD-LIB 217br Stuart Bowey/AD-LIB
218tr Stuart Bowey/AD-LIB

ILLUSTRATION CREDITS

All illustrations are by Janet Jones
except for cat silhouettes and
symbols, which are by Rod
Westblade and Kylie Mulquin.

ACKNOWLEDGMENTS

The publishers wish to thank in particular the following people and organizations
for their assistance in the production of this book: The Cat Clinic, East Chatswood;
Lena Lowe and Matilda, Ferro and Tiddybits; Karen Burgess and Tao; Alex Roche
and Alex Beug and Kin Me; Miriam Coupe; Dr Robyn Nicklin; Alan Walker;
Nancy Katris; Penny Van Peit; Peggy Turvey; Melanie Dabb; Ken and Vickie
Lanham; and Jan and Curt Gabbard.